MACROECONOMICS

A Programmed Book

Third Edition

RICHARD ATTIYEH

University of California, La Jolla

KEITH LUMSDEN

Stanford University

GEORGE LELAND BACH

Stanford University

PRENTICE-HALL, INC., Englewood Cliffs, New Jersey

Printed in the United States of America

10 9 8 7 6 5 4 3 2

0-13-542662-6

Prentice-Hall International, Inc., *London*
Prentice-Hall of Australia, Pty. Ltd., *Sydney*
Prentice-Hall of Canada, Ltd., *Toronto*
Prentice-Hall of India Private Limited, *New Delhi*
Prentice-Hall of Japan, Inc., *Tokyo*

Contents

Preface

Our aim in writing this book and its companion piece *Microeconomics* was to provide students, in a brief period of time, with a working knowledge of basic economics. It was our hope that these two books would prove a valuable tool as the primary reading material in courses that were of short duration (e.g., the one quarter course) or as introductory or supplementary material in more comprehensive courses. Both the reactions of instructors who have used the first editions and the results of a nationwide experiment* designed to evaluate their effectiveness lead us to believe that our objectives have been largely fulfilled. In a study involving 48 colleges and universities, students who read these books as supplementary material scored significantly higher than other students on the Test of Understanding College Economics. Furthermore, and of greater importance, students who spent 12 hours studying either of these books learned as much micro or macroeconomics as students who completed seven weeks on the same topics in a conventional course. On the basis of these results, we reached the following conclusion:

> We feel that these results have important implications for the organization and teaching of the introductory course. Within the profession many believe that the introductory course should prepare a student to think intelligently about major economic problems in modern society and that this goal can best be accomplished by teaching a few basic principles and applying them to a number of important problems. We are in agreement with this view. This study has shown that by using programmed learning

materials the basic micro and macroeconomic theory can be taught in a relatively short period of time. Therefore, more time can be devoted to teaching students how to apply the theory to social problems, both by going more deeply into the more important problems and by actually covering those topics scheduled for the end of the term that often fall victim to the school calendar. The use of these materials can have other advantages: First, the student can gain a good overview of the entire course at the very beginning which helps him to put topics covered in the remainder of the course in meaningful perspective. Second, because a course taught in this manner emphasises the usefulness of economic theory in a problem solving context, it promises a positive impact on the most important single factor in the learning process: namely, student attitude towards the subject.

Much of the increase in flexibility and teaching efficiency afforded by this text stems from its characteristics as a programmed book. A program is designed to develop complex ideas in small, carefully constructed steps. Each step, or frame, requires written responses focussing on key concepts, thereby ensuring continuous participation and involvement by the student. Furthermore, since the correct responses appear at the bottom of each page, it is possible for the student to see immediately whether he is grasping the material, thereby either reinforcing his interest or delineating areas that need further work.

Because of its analytical nature, economics lends itself well to the programming technique. Much of the material in both micro and macroeconomics can be usefully broken down into frames which have desired responses that are both basic and unambiguous. In this text, we develop the simple aggregate demand model of income determination. This model is used to analyze the causes of unemployment and inflation and to show how fiscal and monetary policy can be used to deal with these problems. The student is made aware, however, of the limitations of this model and of the difficulties that can arise in trying to make actual policy decisions. Particular attention is paid to factors such as expectations and market imperfections which might cause a "trade-off" between unemployment and inflation to exist.

In this edition, substantial sections of the book have been rewritten to simplify the presentation and to update the historical record of aggregate economic behavior in the United States. In addition, new review questions have been used at the end of each chapter and a detailed explanation of the correct response to each question has been added.

We are extremely grateful to Michael E. Melody and Cheryl Smith of Prentice-Hall, Inc., for their assistance in preparing this edition for publication.

Richard Attiyeh
Keith Lumsden
George Leland Bach

1

National Output

1.1

In all aspects of life, for individual persons or entire nations, the problem of *scarcity* exists. As an individual, scarcity of time is felt when you find that 24 hours in a day ___*(are/are not)*___ enough to enable you to pursue all the activities you enjoy. Similarly, when the money you have is not sufficient to buy everything you would like to have, you face the problem of ____________.

1.2

These examples make clear that, for an individual, the problem of scarcity exists when his *resources* are not sufficient to satisfy all his wants. If you want to buy and do things, money and time are ______________ that can be used to help satisfy your wants. These resources are *scarce* resources when they ___*(are/are not)*___ sufficient to provide all that you desire.

Answers

1. are not · scarcity
2. resources · are not

1.3

For the nation as a whole, the problem of scarcity takes the same form. A nation's ______________ are not in large enough supply to satisfy all the ______________ of its people. That is, the nation's resources are __________ .

1.4

Economics is the study of the ways individuals and nations cope with the problem of scarcity. In other words, economics is concerned with the use of scarce ______________ to satisfy ______________ .

1.5

When analyzing the behavior of individuals or groups who are confronted with a scarcity problem, economists usually assume that the basic objective is to satisfy wants as fully as possible with the limited supply of resources. That is, it is assumed that individuals and groups try to use their scarce ______________ as efficiently as possible.

1.6

The *efficient* use of scarce resources implies that the *maximum* amount of satisfaction is being obtained from the available supply of resources. However, efficiency *(does/does not)* imply that all wants are satisfied.

1.7

In summary, an economic problem exists whenever resources are ___________. The existence of scarcity means that it is impossible to satisfy all wants with the available supply of ______________ . To obtain the maximum possible satisfaction with those resources, they must be used ______________ .

Answers

3. resources · wants · scarce
4. resources · wants
5. resources
6. does not
7. scarce · resources · efficiently

1.8

Economic activity, then, is the attempt to convert a limited supply of resources into a bundle of commodities (goods and services) that gives ____*(more/less)*____ satisfaction than any other bundle that can be obtained with those resources.

When this goal is achieved, resources are being allocated or used ____________.

1.9

When considering an entire nation, it is clear that the level of economic welfare attained depends on two factors:

a. the quantity of ______________ available, and

b. how ______________ these resources are used.

1.10

The more resources an economy has and the more efficiently those resources are used, the ____*(larger/smaller)*____ will be the *output* of commodities that can be produced in a year. The larger the output that an economy can produce in a year, the ____*(more/less)*____ fully will its consumers be able to satisfy their wants.

1.11

Unfortunately, it is impossible to measure directly the level of satisfaction or *economic welfare* attained by the consumers of an economy. As a result, economists use the amount of output produced in a year as an indicator of

______________ welfare. For example, it is impossible to say how much more satisfied consumers are this year than last, but it is possible to say how much more ______________ is available to consumers this year compared with last year.

1.12

Total output can be calculated in several ways. For example, two possibilities are to count the number of things produced or to measure the weight of those things produced. Whatever calculation is made, however, it is desirable that it provide a guide for measuring the economic ______________ of consumers.

Answers

8. more · efficiently
9. resources · efficiently
10. larger · more
11. economic · output
12. welfare

1.13

If there were only one commodity produced, there would be little difficulty in measuring the annual output of an economy. If that commodity were hot dogs, for instance, the annual ______________ could be measured simply by either the number or weight of hot dogs produced in one ______________. Either measure would enable one to determine whether economic welfare was increasing or decreasing from year to year.

1.14

But because there are many commodities produced in an economy, calculating total ______________ by simply adding up the number or weight of items produced will not provide a good measure of economic ______________.

1.15

Even if there were only two commodities produced, the simple counting procedure would not work well. Suppose the two commodities were hot dogs and hot rods. Assume production for the past two years was as follows:

	This Year	*Last Year*
Hot Dogs	1,000	2,000
Hot Rods	500	5

In which year was output greater? The simple counting procedure would indicate that output was greater ______________ year. But, because most people consider a hot rod to represent considerably more output than a hot dog, they would say that output was greater ______________ year. If you were to spend a year in this economy, in which year would you choose to be there: one like this year or one like last year? This example makes clear that when there is more than one kind of commodity produced, the number of units produced ___*(is/is not)*___ generally a useful measure of output.

Answers

13. output · year
14. output · welfare
15. last · this · is not

1.16

What is a good measure? Consider the possibility of using weight as a measure. Suppose that the only two commodities are bread and bricks and that weight is used as a measure of output. Because a brick is much heavier than a loaf of bread, an economy that produced very few loaves of bread but many bricks would appear to have a lot ___*(more/less)*___ output than an economy that produced many loaves of bread but few bricks. This would result from using

______________ as a measure of output, even if the economy with more bread and fewer bricks satisfied consumers' wants more fully.

1.17

The difficulty with using either number of items or weight as a measure of output is that neither is a good guide to the amount of satisfaction different commodities give to customers. One beautiful painting may give more satisfaction

than many jelly beans or a ton of sand. To measure ______________ in this example by either the number or the weight of goods produced ___*(does/does not)*___ generally provide a good measure of economic welfare.

1.18

In constructing a measure of output that is a meaningful guide to the level of economic welfare, it is desirable that the importance attached to each item produced be in proportion to its *value* to consumers. In terms of a previous example, if consumers consider a load of bread to be more valuable to them than a brick, then a loaf of bread should be considered to be a ___*(larger/smaller)*___ amount of output than a brick.

1.19

Suppose that consumers consider a loaf of bread to be ten times as valuable as a brick. Further suppose that the production of bricks and bread for the last two years were as follows:

	This Year	*Last Year*
Bread	200 million	100 million
Bricks	500 million	900 million

Answers

16. more · weight
17. output · does not
18. larger

If output should be measured to reflect its value to consumers, in which year was output greater? Because consumers consider a loaf of bread to be ten times as valuable as a brick, ______________ year's output was greater. This is true even though the weight and number of the items produced were greater __________ year.

1.20
To be useful as a guide to the level of economic welfare, an output measure should count each item produced in proportion to the ______________ attached to it by consumers.

1.21
For an economy like that of the United States, with millions of commodities and millions of consumers, this seems an impossible task. Nevertheless, information on the way consumers value different commodities is readily available. This information makes it possible to construct a measure of ______________ that counts each commodity in proportion to the value given it by __________.

1.22
In order to discover where to find this information, consider the spending behavior of a typical consumer who tries to allocate his *income* among different commodities in order to satisfy his ______________ as fully as possible.

1.23
What commodities a consumer can and will buy depends, among other things, on what he must pay for them. What he must pay for a unit of any commodity is called the *price* of that commodity. The way in which a consumer spends his income depends on the ______________ of different commodities.

1.24
In deciding how to spend your income each week, many factors will influence your decisions. Among these are the size of your income, your tastes and prefer-

Answers

19. this · last
20. value
21. output · consumers
22. wants
23. prices

ences, and perhaps even the weather. But given all of these factors, before you decide how to allocate or spend your ______________ among different commodities, you would like to know the ______________ of each commodity.

1.25

For example, given the prices of all other commodities, if the price of a movie ticket is $5, you will most likely use your income to see movies *(more/less)* often and buy *(more/less)* of other commodities than you would if the price were 50 cents.

1.26

If the price is 50 cents, you may well go to the movies four times a month, whereas at a price of $5 you will go only once a month. In other words, at different prices you will have different expenditure patterns. At 50 cents per ticket the second, third, and fourth movies *(will/will not)* be worth seeing; at $5 per ticket they *(will/will not)* be worth seeing.

1.27

As long as you try to spend your income wisely, you will not continue to buy things that *(are/are not)* worth to you what you must pay for them. You will adjust your expenditure pattern when there are changes in the ______________ of commodities to avoid buying what is not worth its price to you.

1.28

For this reason, it can be expected that the ______________ paid for different commodities will reflect their *values* to consumers.

1.29

When the price of a movie ticket is $5, if you go to one movie it must be that the ______________ of that movie to you is at least $5. When the price of a movie ticket is 50 cents, if you go to four movies it can be inferred that the __________ of a movie to you is at least 50 cents.

Answers

24. income · price
25. less · more
26. will · will not
27. are not · prices
28. prices
29. value · value

1.30

In constructing a measure of output that would serve as a useful guide to the level of economic welfare, it is necessary to have information on the __________ of different commodities to consumers. Information on the values of different commodities to consumers can be found in the ______________ of these commodities.

1.31

How can prices be used to construct a measure of total output produced in a year? If prices of different commodities reflect their relative importance to consumers, then a unit of any commodity can be measured by its ______________. The total output of any commodity would then be the number of units times the ______________ per unit.

1.32

The total output of all commodities would be the sum of the total outputs of the individual commodities. For the brick-bread economy, output would be calculated as follows: (fill in the missing numbers)

This Year

	Quantity	*Price*	*Output*
Bread	200 million	$.25	$50 million
Bricks	500 million	.05	25 million
Total Output			____ million

Last Year

	Quantity	*Price*	*Output*
Bread	100 million	$.25	$ ____ million
Bricks	900 million	.05	____ million
Total Output			____ million

Answers

30. value · prices
31. price · price
32. 75 · 25 · 45 · 70

1.33

Counting each commodity in proportion to its value in the market, output was greater ______________ year.

1.34

The reason market values of the production of different commodities are used as measures of their output is that the ______________ of these commodities reflect their values to consumers.

1.35

By weighing each unit of a commodity by its price, instead of in pounds and ounces, a measure of output is obtained that counts each commodity in proportion to the value placed on it by ______________ .

1.36

Thus, by counting each commodity as it is valued in the market—that is, by multiplying the quantity of the commodity by its ______________ —a measure of total output is obtained that serves as a guide to the level of economic welfare in the economy.

1.37

The procedure of measuring total ______________ by the market value of the goods and services produced underlies the official national output statistics for the United States. But for a complex economy like that of the United States, there are a number of difficulties that are not apparent in the hypothetical brick-bread economy but that must be overcome before an accurate measure of total ______________ can be obtained.

1.38

To understand two of the major problems in constructing a measure of total output, consider the output of just three commodities: automobiles, automobile-producing machinery, and steel. To simplify matters, suppose that steel is used

Answers

33. this
34. prices
35. consumers
36. price
37. output · output

only to produce automobiles and automobile-producing machinery, and that the market value of these commodities produced this year was as follows:

Market value of steel produced	$10 billion
Market value of auto machinery produced	0 billion
Market value of automobiles produced	30 billion
Note: Market value of steel used in automobiles	8 billion

From these data, you know that some of the steel produced was used in the production of ______________. Because $10 billion of steel was produced and only $8 billion was used in the production of automobiles, $ ______________ billion must have been stored for use in the future. You also see that the amount of automobile-producing machinery produced this year was ______________.

1.39

Because steel is used up in the production of automobiles, part of the market value of automobiles comes from the value of the steel used. For this reason, if the total output of these three commodities is obtained by adding up their separate market values, part of the output of ______________ will be counted twice, once in its own market value and again as part of the ______________ ______________ of automobiles.

1.40

If we add together the market value of the steel used in the automobiles and the market value of the automobiles, we will be including the value of the steel twice. This is known as *double counting* because we are including the value of steel ______________. In the above example, simply adding up the market values for all commodities would give a calculated output of $ ______________ billion, but this would overstate total production by $ ______________ billion because of ______________ counting.

Answers

38. automobiles · 2 · zero
39. steel · market value
40. twice · 40 · 8 · double

1.41

Commodities used to produce other commodities during the same period in which they themselves are produced are called *intermediate* goods. Steel is an example of an ______________ good because during the period in which it was produced it was used up in the production of automobiles. All other commodities are called *final* goods. Automobiles are ______________ goods because they *(are/are not)* used up in the production of other goods in the period in which they are produced.

1.42

It is possible for part of the production of a commodity to be counted as an intermediate good and part as a final good. In this example, part of the year's production of steel was used up in the production of automobiles and part was stored for future use. The part used up would be counted as an ______________ good and the part stored as a ______________ good. Of the total production of steel, $ ______________ billion would be counted as an intermediate good and $ ______________ billion as a final good.

1.43

Because the market value of final goods includes the market value of the intermediate goods, one way to avoid ______________ counting would be to exclude from the calculation of total output all ______________ goods. The justification for such an exclusion is that those goods are already counted in the output of the ______________ goods that they helped to produce.

1.44

Thus, the definition of *total output* should be modified to be the market value of all ______________ goods produced during the time period under consideration. In the example, then, total output would be calculated as follows:

Answers

41. intermediate · final · are not
42. intermediate · final · 8 · 2
43. double · intermediate · final
44. final

Final output of steel	$ ______________	billion
Final output of auto machinery	______________	billion
Final output of automobiles	______________	billion
Total output of these commodities	32	billion

1.45

That this calculation is sensible can be seen by the answer to the following question: What has the sum total of productive activity this year made available to society for its present use or for use in the future? The answer is: $______________ billion worth of automobiles, $ ______________ billion worth of steel to be used in the future, or a total output of $ ______________ billion.

1.46

The same measure of total output can be derived in a different manner by answering this question: What is the *value added* to total output by each industry during the year? In the example, it is most useful to start by considering the automobile industry. During the year, the automobile industry acquired $ ______________ billion worth of steel produced this year and converted it into $ ______________ billion worth of automobiles. In the process, there was $ ______________ billion of value ______________ to total output by the auto industry.

1.47

In the auto machinery industry, there was no production, so there was zero ______________ ______________ by that industry. In the steel industry, the value added to the total output was $ ______________ billion.

1.48

Thus, total output can be calculated by summing the ______________ ______________ by each industry. This method will yield the same result as summing the market value of all ______________ goods produced.

Answers

44. 2 · 0 · 30
45. 30 · 2 · 32
46. 8 · 30 · 22 · added
47. value added · 10
48. value added · final

1.49

The first of the two problems, then, is how to avoid the error of ____________ ____________, which can result when some commodities are used in the production of others during the period for which output is being calculated. The solution to this problem is to measure output by either the market value of all ____________ ____________ produced or ____________ ____________ by all industries.

1.50

Consider now the second problem. In the production of automobiles, it is necessary to use automobile-producing machinery as well as steel. In this example, the value of auto machinery produced was $ ____________ billion. Because machines were produced in earlier years, machinery *(is/is not)* available for use even though no new machinery was produced this year.

1.51

In the process of producing automobiles, machinery both becomes older and incurs a certain amount of wear and tear. Both these factors lead to a *(rise/decline)* in the value of the machinery. This change in the value of machinery and other capital goods due to aging and wear and tear is called *depreciation.*

1.52

The reduction in the value of *capital goods,* which is called ____________, reflects the fact that the older capital goods are and the more they have been used, the *(more/less)* output they are capable of producing.

1.53

In calculating the total amount of output produced in the economy, it is important to take into account the ____________ that accrues on the capital goods needed to produce the output.

Answers

49. double counting · final goods · value added
50. 0 · is
51. decline
52. depreciation · less
53. depreciation

1.54

Thus, to have a complete account of the gain from productive activity during any period, the depreciation on the capital goods that has occurred during that period should be *(added to/subtracted from)* the market value of the final goods produced.

1.55

Failure to deduct depreciation in the calculation of total output is similar to the mistake of double counting. Depreciation can be thought of as the amount of ______________ goods used up in the production of current output. In this way, capital goods are like intermediate goods, except that ______________ goods are produced in the same period they are used up, whereas ______________ goods are produced in earlier periods.

1.56

Because the value of any capital good was counted as part of total output for the year in which it was produced, failure to deduct the part of that capital good used up in current production would be to count that part of the ______________ good a second time. In other words, when ______________ is not deducted from current output, it means that some output, produced in an earlier period, is counted again as part of current output.

1.57

Because depreciation cannot be observed directly, it is difficult to measure accurately, and comparisons of output for different years may be distorted by changes in the way depreciation is measured. As a result, many economists consider the value of output produced without a deduction for depreciation to be a better basis for comparisons over time. For this reason, the official statistics report total output both ways: with and without a deduction for ______________.

Answers

54. subtracted from
55. capital · intermediate · capital
56. capital · depreciation
57. depreciation

1.58

The value of total output for an economy in a year *without* a deduction for depreciation is termed the *gross national product,* frequently abbreviated GNP. The value of that output *with* a deduction for depreciation is *net national product,* or NNP. Of course, NNP + ______________ = GNP. For the reasons cited above, the most commonly used measure of output is GNP, even though ____________ is conceptually preferable for many purposes.

1.59

Both GNP and NNP measure the market ______________ of all the final goods and services produced in a given period of time. The only difference is that ______________ does not include a deduction for depreciation, whereas ______________ does.

1.60

Following custom, much of the analysis in this book will be in terms of GNP. However, you should be aware that, although for most purposes it makes little difference which measure of total output is used, ______________ is preferred by reason of statistical accuracy, and ______________ is preferred by reason of conceptual correctness. Thus, the second problem of how to account for the capital goods used up in production cannot be completely solved because of data limitations.

1.61

In summary, the measurement of output is an attempt to quantify the level of economic well-being. In seeking to satisfy their wants, the members of an economy use their ______________ to produce commodities. Because resources are ______________, not all wants can be completely satisfied. But when resources are used ______________, wants will be satisfied as fully as possible with the available supply of resources.

Answers

58. depreciation · NNP
59. value · GNP · NNP
60. GNP · NNP
61. resources · scarce · efficiently

1.62

In adding up the amount of output produced, it is necessary, because there are many different commodities, to determine the relative importance of each. In a market economy, the ______________ of different commodities can be taken as indicators of the relative values of these commodities to consumers.

1.63

The use of ______________ to measure the relative importance of different commodities leads to a measure of output that is the market value of all ______________ goods and services produced in a year.

1.64

Total output is the market value of final goods and services only because the market value of ______________ goods is included in the market value of the final goods. To add up the market value of all commodities would result in ______________ ______________ of intermediate goods and services.

1.65

Related to the problem of double counting of intermediate goods is the problem of the capital goods used up in the production of output. This loss in value of capital goods is called ______________. To obtain an accurate measure of the gain to society from its total economic activity, it is necessary to *(add/subtract)* ______________ depreciation from the market value of final goods and services produced.

1.66

But because depreciation is very hard to measure accurately, the market value of output without a deduction for depreciation is commonly used for making comparisons over time. This measure is called ______________. It is sometimes preferred to ______________ because it is statiscally more accurate even though it is conceptually less desirable.

Answers

62. prices
63. prices · final
64. intermediate · double counting
65. depreciation · subtract
66. GNP · NNP

REVIEW QUESTIONS

At the end of each chapter, there will be a set of review questions to test your comprehension of the material and to set you thinking about some of its implications. Many of these questions are difficult. Before you decide on an answer, be sure you have read all·the possible answers and understand not only why your answer is correct but also why the other answers are wrong. To help make these questions a useful learning device, a suggested explanation of the correct response is provided for each question. Be sure to circle the response you believe is correct before you read the explanation. Whenever you choose an incorrect response, do not go on until you understand where you made your mistake.

1.1
It is said that the United States is "an economy of scarcity." This statement:

a. is ridiculous, because the United States is the richest country the world has ever known.
b. is ridiculous, because the resources that are scarce in the United States can always be imported from abroad.
c. is true, because our resources are not sufficient to allow us to realize all our goals.
d. is true, but only temporarily—in the decade of the 1980s we will probably have adequate resources to achieve our goals.

Scarcity exists when there are not sufficient resources to produce all the goods and services consumers want. Even though the United States might be rich in comparison to other countries, it is not true that it has sufficient resources to produce everything that the American people want. Obviously, we would like to have better hospitals, more parks, cleaner air, and so on. Nor is it true that we can get all we want by importing resources from other countries or by accumulating more resources for use in the future. We probably can never eliminate scarcity. The correct response is c.

1.2
Last year, a small island economy produced only the following commodities:

$150,000 worth of fish
$ 35,000 worth of bait
$ 20,000 worth of nets

During the year, $10,000 worth of nets became damaged and had to be discarded. For this economy, which of the following is true?

a. GNP and NNP were $205,000 and $215,000, respectively.
b. GNP and NNP were $170,000 and $160,000, respectively.
c. GNP and NNP were $205,000 and $195,000, respectively.
d. GNP and NNP cannot be derived from the above information.

The final consumption good in the island economy is fish, and thus the $150,000 worth of fish enters both GNP and NNP. The bait is an intermediate good assisting in the "production" of fish, and the value of output includes the output of bait. Nets are investment goods. Of the $20,000 worth of nets produced, $10,000 worth wear out or are used up in the production process. Thus, during the year, the output of final goods was $150,000 worth of fish and the $20,000 worth of nets. GNP, therefore, was $170,000. Depreciation was $10,000; thus, NNP was $160,000. The correct response is b.

1.3

If you were to add up all the sales in the economy for a given year, which of the following would be true with respect to the grand total for that year?

a. It would equal GNP.
b. It would exceed GNP.
c. It would be less than GNP.
d. It would ignore consumers' valuation of the goods and services produced.

Adding together all sales in the economy would be double counting. For instance, the sale of wheat would be added to the sale of flour, which would be added to the sale of the final loaf of bread–the wheat would be included three times in the examples. Thus, the sum would exceed GNP. The rational buyer's purchases, however, whether he be a miller or baker or bread buyer would reflect his valuations of the commodity. The correct response is b.

1.4

Which of the following statements about gross national product would be correct?

1. GNP uses prices as weights in adding together the outputs of different goods and services.
2. GNP includes depreciation as part of output.
3. GNP is the market value of all final goods and services produced.

a. 1 and 2 only
b. 1 and 3 only
c. 2 and 3 only
d. 1, 2, and 3

Gross national product is defined as the market value of all final goods and services produced, where the phrase "final goods and services" means all those goods and services not used up in the production of other goods and services during the period for which output is being measured. Consequently, statement 3 is correct. The market value of the output of any good is equal to the price of the good times the quantity produced. This means that in adding together the market value of all goods and services the quantity of each good and service is counted in proportion to its price. Consequently, statement 1 is correct. Because GNP does include a deduction for the decrease in the value of capital goods that occurs during the period of measurement, statement 2 is correct. The correct response is d.

2

Expenditure and Income

2.1

Total output, as measured by GNP, is the ________________ ________________ of all final goods and services produced in a year. Most output is sold by its producers to consumers, other businesses, or governments. To this extent, output is matched by *expenditure* for ________________ goods and services.

2.2

Because most output is sold in the marketplace, that part of output is equal in value to the ________________ made for it. But what about output, produced by businesses that does not get sold in the period for which output is measured?

2.3

Goods that are produced by a business but not sold to consumers, other businesses, or governments are classified as *inventories*. When producers accumulate inventories of their own product, they are considered to purchase the goods from

Answers

1. market value · final
2. expenditure

themselves. As a result, it is assumed that even output that takes the form of

_______________ is matched by an expenditure of an equal amount.

2.4

As a result, total output—that is, the market value of all _______________

goods and services—is matched by an equal amount of _______________ for those goods and services.

2.5

As will be seen in subsequent chapters, it is useful for many purposes to classify final product according to the type of purchaser. Thus, GNP is frequently re-

ferred to as the sum of all _______________ for final goods and services made by consumers, businesses, and governments. For 1972, GNP was broken down as follows:

Type of Purchaser	*Type of Expenditure*	*Amount*
Consumers	Consumption	$721 billion
Businesses	Investment	176 billion
Governments	Government	255 billion
		$1,152 billion

2.6

As these tables show, expenditure by consumers is termed _______________

and accounts for the *(largest/smallest)* portion of total expenditure for final goods and services.

2.7

Expenditure by businesses is termed _______________. This category includes expenditure for items such as plant, equipment, and inventories. The essential characteristic of investment expenditure is that it leads to a use of output that does not provide for the satisfaction of consumers' wants in the present, but en-

larges the possibility for satisfying _______________ wants in the future.

Answers

3. inventories
4. final · expenditure
5. expenditures
6. consumption · largest
7. investment · consumers'

2.8

Expenditure for plant and equipment increases the productive capacity of businesses to produce in the ________________. The accumulation of inventories represents the putting aside of goods produced in the present period that can be used in the ________________.

2.9

The third category of expenditure is ________________ expenditure. This type of expenditure includes any purchase of a good or service by a government (federal, state, or local). Expenditure for highway construction or public school education *(would/would not)* fall into this category.

2.10

All three types of expenditure include only purchases of final ________________ and ________________. That is, consumption, investment, and government expenditures are defined as outlays for output produced in the current period.

2.11

The purchase of a used automobile by a consumer *(would/would not)* be included in consumption expenditure, because it is not an outlay for currently produced output. Such a transaction does not reflect the creation of a good or service to satisfy wants, but merely the transfer of *(a new/an existing)* commodity from one person to another.

2.12

Similarly, the purchase of common stock cannot be considered investment expenditure because it is *not* the purchase of newly produced ________________ that provides for greater future comsumption. Again this transaction simply represents the *(transfer/production)* of an already existing item from the seller to the buyer.

Answers

8. future · future
9. government · would
10. goods · services (either order)
11. would not · an existing
12. output (goods) · transfer

2.13

As with consumers and businesses, not all outlays by the government are expenditure for newly produced final goods and services. Many items in government budgets are *transfer payments* from the government to private persons or groups, such as welfare payments to poor persons. The purchase of a missile would be included in ______________ ______________, whereas social security benefits are ______________ ______________.

2.14

In any year, total output, which is measured by the market value of all ______________ goods and services produced, equals the total ______________ for final goods and services by consumers, businesses, and governments.

2.15

Previously, it was pointed out that total output is also measured by the sum of ______________ added in the production of each commodity, including both final and intermediate goods. Value added in the production of a commodity is the value of that commodity minus the value of the ______________ goods used in its production.

2.16

For example, the value added in the production of bread is the ______________ of the bread minus the value of the ______________ goods, such as flour, yeast, and so on, used to make bread. The value added in the production of flour is the value of the ______________ minus the value of the intermediate goods, such as wheat, used up in the production of flour.

2.17

The sum of the value added in the production of all commodities (including both final and intermediate goods) and the market value of all ______________ goods are equivalent measures of total output.

Answers

13. government expenditure · transfer payments
14. final · expenditure
15. value · intermediate
16. value · intermediate · flour
17. final

2.18

Consider the following accounts of a hypothetical furniture producer:

Receipts		*Payments*	
Sales	$20,000	Lumber, paint, etc.	$ 7,000
		Wages and salaries	6,000
		Interest	500
		Rent	500
		Depreciation	2,000
		Total costs	$16,000
		Profit (receipts-costs)	4,000
Total receipts	$20,000	Total payments	$20,000

The first point to notice is that total receipts and total payments are

_______________ . Total receipts and payments not only *are* equal they *must* be equal. The reason is that one type of payment, *profit,* is defined as total receipts minus total costs. As a result, all payments, including profit,

taken together must add up to total _______________ . All that this means is that an owner of a business can pay himself the amount of receipts left over

after all _______________ have been paid.

2.19

Because total receipts and total payments must, by definition, be equal, it is possible for profit to be either positive or negative. If total costs are greater than total receipts, for example, profit must be *(positive/negative)* .

2.20

From the accounts of the furniture producer, it is possible to calculate the value added by this business. The value added is equal to the value of the goods

produced less the value of the _______________ goods used up.

Answers

18. equal (both $20,000) · receipts · costs
19. negative
20. intermediate

2.21

The value added for this firm is the value of output produced ($ __________) minus the value of the intermediate goods ($ __________), which equals $ __________.

2.22

The accounts of this firm can be reconstructed to show its value added by subtracting from both receipts and payments the value of the __________ goods used in production as follows:

Sales	$20,000	Wages and salaries	$ 6,000
Less: purchases of intermediate goods	7,000	Rent	500
		Interest	500
		Depreciation	2,000
		Profit	4,000
Value added	$13,000	Income payments	$13,000

2.23

In the value added accounts, the purchases of lumber, paint, and so on are no longer included. The receipts side shows the value added by the producer, which is the market value of the furniture produced minus the market value of the __________ goods used. Of the total value of furniture produced, *(all/only part)* originates in the furniture business and *(none/the rest)* originates in the lumber, paint, and other intermediate goods businesses.

2.24

The payments side shows only *income* payments. These are payments made to the owners of the resources used to create the value added. Wages and salaries are __________ payments made to persons who provide labor services by working for this business.

Answers

21. 20,000 · 7,000 · 13,000
22. intermediate
23. intermediate · only part · the rest
24. income

2.25

Rent is an ______________ payment made to the owners of land and capital goods that have been rented or leased by this firm.

2.26

Interest is an ______________ payment that is part of the return to the land and capital goods that were bought by the owner of the business. In order to pay for these resources, it was necessary to borrow money. In return for their loans, the lenders receive part of the income earned by the owner's land and capital goods. This income is called ______________ .

2.27

Depreciation is the ______________ payment received by the owner of the business in return for the wear and tear on his capital goods.

2.28

The remaining income payment made by this firm is called ______________ . This is the reward to the owner for investing and risking his wealth in the business. Like wages, salaries, rent, interest, and depreciation, profit is a type of ______________ payment.

2.29

As the totals make clear, the value added and the total income payments are ______________ . This equality results from the fact that any part of total receipts not paid out in costs is taken as profit by the owner of the business in return for the resources he provides. In other words, all the value added by this business is equal to the income payments made in return for the use of the ______________ that create that value.

Answers

25. income
26. income · interest
27. income
28. profit · income
29. equal · resources

2.30

Thus, for each business it is true that the _______________ added equals total _______________ payments. Adding together the value added by all producers gives total output. At the same time, adding together the incomes paid by all producers gives total income. As a result, for the economy as a whole total output must be equal to total _______________ .

2.31

It has just been shown that for the economy as a whole total output and total income *(must/can)* be equal because all the value added by each producer is paid out as different types of _______________ , including the _______________ received by the owners of the businesses in return for the resources that they provide.

2.32

Most businesses must pay certain taxes, such as sales and property taxes, that are not based on income earned. These are called *indirect business taxes*—because they do not tax incomes directly. In the furniture example, the firm had to make _______________ payments for the use of resources, but it did not have to pay _______________ _______________ taxes.

2.33

Suppose that the furniture producer did have to pay indirect business taxes—for example, property taxes of $1,000. In this case, his value added accounts would appear this way:

Sales	$20,000	Income payments	$12,000
Less: purchases of intermediate goods	7,000	Indirect business taxes	1,000
Value added	$13,000		$13,000

In this case, the value added equals income payments for resources plus _______________ _______________ _______________ .

Answers

30. value · income · income
31. must · income · profit
32. income · indirect business
33. indirect business taxes

2.34

For the economy as a whole, then, total output equals the sum of all ________ payments plus ____________ ____________ taxes.

2.35

Previously, it was argued that for the economy as a whole total ____________ produced and total ____________ earned are equal.

2.36

But is has just been shown that when there are indirect business taxes, some of the value added *(does/does not)* get paid to the resources used. As a result, the total income paid falls short of the value of output by the amount of

____________ ____________ ____________.

2.37

As the name given to these taxes suggests, however, even though these taxes are not based on income, they do constitute an ____________ tax on income. All resources taken together do "earn" an income equal to the value of total ____________, but they are not paid all that income because some is claimed by the government in the form of sales, property, and similar taxes.

2.38

Thus, counting both the income actually paid for resources and the income taxed indirectly, the basic result that total output and total income are ____________ holds true.

2.39

In this chapter, two fundamental equalities have been identified. One is the equality between total output and total expenditure. The other is the equality

Answers

34. income · indirect business
35. output · income
36. does not · indirect business taxes
37. indirect · output
38. equal

of total output and total income. The importance of the fact that total output is equal to both total ______________ and total ______________ is that it makes it possible to consider the rate of economic activity from two different points of view.

2.40

In any given year, the total output of an economy (GNP) can be measured in two ways that yield *(the same/a different)* result. Just as it is possible to identify a penny by either its head or tail side, so it is possible to measure GNP by either total ______________ or total ______________ .

2.41

Consider the illustration below.

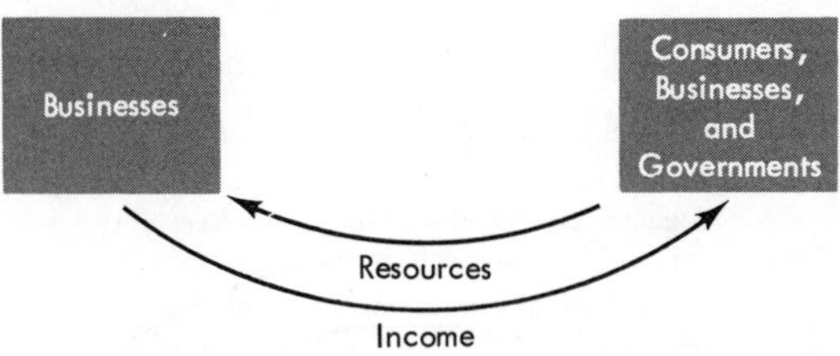

Resource owners provide businesses with resources in return for payments called ______________ . The most common transaction of this type in our economy is the payment of ______________ to consumers for labor services. Another example is the payment of rent to another business for the use of its building.

2.42

Thus, in the simplified diagram above, there is a flow of resources from their owners to ______________ and a flow of ______________ in the opposite direction from businesses to resource owners.

Answers

39. expenditure · income (either order)
40. the same · expenditure · income (either order)
41. income · wages (income)
42. businesses · income

2.43

Now look at the following illustration.

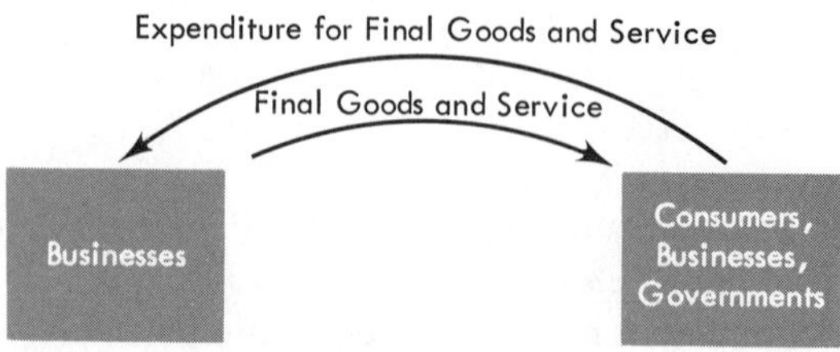

This illustration shows a flow of ______________ goods and services in return for the ______________ made for them.

2.44

Combining both illustrations, the circular flow of income and expenditure becomes apparent.

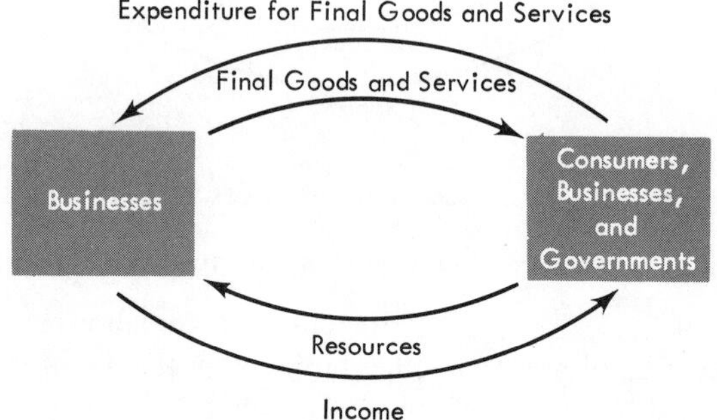

Income is earned in the production of output and in turn is used to make ______________ for that output. At the same time, expenditure for output provides the funds with which businesses make ______________ payments.

Answers

43. final · expenditure
44. expenditure · income

2.45

Because GNP is defined as the market value of final goods and services, it is equal both to total ______________ for final goods and services by consumers, businesses, and governments and to total ______________ earned by the owners of resources used in production.

2.46

The following table shows for 1972 both the expenditure and income flows that took place as a consequence of producing the ______________ for that year.

U. S. NATIONAL EXPENDITURE AND INCOME, 1972 (BILLIONS OF DOLLARS)

Expenditure		*Income*	
Consumption	721	Compensation of employees	705
Investment	176	Rents	26
Government	255	Interest	41
		Depreciation	104
		Profits and other business income	166
		Indirect business taxes	110
		Statistical discrepancy	0
Total expenditure (GNP)	1,152	Total income (GNP)	1,152

2.47

Both total expenditure and total income are equivalent measures of an economy's ______________. As a result, by considering either the expenditure or income side of this table it is possible to determine that the market value of final goods and services produced in the United States in 1972 was $ ______________ billion.

Answers

45. expenditure · income
46. GNP (output)
47. GNP (output) · 1,152

2.48

Because of the many receipts and payments that must be tabulated to produce the results shown in the above table, it should not come as a surprise that there will be some error in measuring expenditure and income. Because of this error, measured total expenditure and total income are not exactly equal, even though the true values for these two flows must be ________________. This error of measurement, which is usually quite small, is shown on the income side of the table as the statistical discrepancy. In 1972, the statistical discrepancy was $ ________________ billion.

2.49

The other items shown on the income side represent the earnings of the different factors of production used to produce output in 1972. As the first entry shows, in return for providing labor services employees were paid, mostly in the form of wages and salaries, in the amount of ________________ billion. The next four items on the income side show how the payments for nonlabor resources were allocated among different types of capital income receipts.

2.50

Not all income, however, is available to the owners of resources to spend as they like. For example, as was discussed earlier in this chapter indirect business ________________ represent income that was earned by resources but that was never paid to their owners. This income is taken by the ________________ in the form of sales, property, and certain other taxes before resource owners receive it.

2.51

In addition to indirect business taxes, the government also takes income away from individuals by taxing their income directly. Direct personal taxes are another example of ________________ that individuals earn but do not keep to ________________ as they choose.

Answers

48. equal · 0
49. 705 · 26
50. taxes · government
51. income · spend

2.52

The government affects the amount of income that individuals have to spend in a way other than collecting taxes. One of the uses of government tax revenue is to supplement the income of certain people with *transfer payments.* Taxes are payments from individuals to the _______________, and transfer payments are made by the government to _______________.

2.53

To calculate how much income consumers have to make consumption expenditure, it is necessary to subtract the amount households pay in _______________ and add the amount they receive in _______________ _______________.

2.54

As in the case with consumers, not all the income received by businesses is retained by businesses. Some of it is paid to the government in the form of direct business _______________. The higher business taxes are, the lower will be the amount of income that _______________ have to spend as they like.

2.55

In addition to taxes, businesses usually pay part of the income they earn to their owners, in the form of *dividends.* When a business pays _______________ to its owners (who, of course, are individual consumers), the spendable income of businesses goes ___*(up/down*___, while that of consumers goes ___*(up/down)*___.

2.56

To determine how much income businesses have available to make investment expenditure, it is necessary to take into account the amounts they pay to the government in the form of _______________ and to consumers in the form of _______________.

Answers

52. government · individuals
53. taxes · transfer payments
54. taxes · businesses
55. dividends · down · up
56. taxes · dividends

2.57

Even though governments do not receive income in return for providing resources for use in production, they do have income to spend because of the various ______________ they collect. Not all tax receipts, however, are available for purchases of goods and services, because some are used to supplement the income of consumers in the form of ______________ payments.

2.58

The income that governments can use for government expenditure is equal to ______________ receipts minus ______________ payments.

2.59

In the preceding table showing expenditure and income flows, total income was divided into different types of income, such as wages and salaries, rent, and so on. For some purposes, it is useful to divide total income into the amounts available to consumers to make ______________ expenditure, to businesses to make ______________ expenditure, and to the government to make ________ expenditure.

2.60

The income that consumers have available to spend is called *disposable income.* Previously, it was noted that ______________ income is equal to the income paid to individuals plus the income paid to consumers by businesses in the form of ______________ less the income paid by consumers to governments in the form of ______________ plus the income paid to consumers by governments in the form of ______________ ______________ .

2.61

The income that businesses can spend is called *retained earnings.* Retained ______________ , of course, is equal to depreciation, profits, and other

Answers

57. taxes · transfer
58. tax · transfer
59. consumption · investment · government
60. disposable · dividends · taxes · transfer payments
61. earnings

business income minus _______________ paid to the government minus _______________ paid to consumers.

2.62

The income available to governments is called *net taxes,* which is equal to total _______________ paid to the government minus government _______________ _______________ to consumers.

2.63

These definitions of the spendable income of consumers, businesses and governments is shown in the following table.

wages, salaries, interest, rents + dividends − direct personal taxes + transfer payments	=	_______________ _______________
profit, other business income + depreciation − direct business taxes − dividends	=	_______________ _______________
indirect business taxes + direct personal taxes + direct business taxes − transfer payments	=	_______________ _______________

2.64

Because all total income must show up as the spendable income for one or another sector of the economy, the sum of disposable income, retained earnings, and net taxes must add up to total _______________, or GNP.

Answers

61. taxes · dividends
62. taxes · transfer payments
63. disposable income · retained earnings · net taxes
64. output

2.65
The following table shows expenditure and income for 1972 with the new breakdown of income into spendable income by sector.

U. S. NATIONAL EXPENDITURE AND INCOME, 1972 (BILLIONS OF DOLLARS)

Expenditure		*Income*	
Consumption	721	Disposable income	776
Investment	176	Retained earnings	127
Government	255	Net taxes	249
		Statistical discrepancy	0
Total expenditure (GNP)	1,152	Total income (GNP)	1,152

As this table shows, after allowing for the statistical discrepancy, both the

_______________ made by consumers, businesses, and governments and the

_______________ that these groups have available to spend was equal to

_______________.

REVIEW QUESTIONS

2.1
For any particular receipt to be counted as part of an economy's total income, which of the following must be true?

a. It must be in return for a good or service.
b. It must be in return for the use of resources in the production of current output.
c. It must represent repayment for a loan.
d. It must represent an increase in the welfare of the recipient.

GNP is the total money expenditures for final goods and services produced. Total income, which by definition must equal GNP, is the total income flow to resource owners whose resources produced all the final goods and services. For any particular receipt, therefore, to be included in total income, it must be a

Answers

65. expenditure · income · GNP ($1,152)

return for the use of resources in the production of current output. The correct response is b.

2.2

For the economy as a whole, which of the following is correct with respect to investment expenditure?

a. It does not benefit consumers.
b. It makes possible higher levels of consumption in the future.
c. It is primarily the purchase of stocks and bonds.
d. It is part of GNP but not NNP.

Investment expenditure, by increasing the stock of capital in the economy, increases potential GNP and consequently makes possible higher levels of consumption in the future. Thus, it benefits consumers. The difference between GNP and NNP is capital depreciation–both include new investment as well as C + G. However, *investment*, as you now use the word, that is, creation of new capital, does not mean swapping money for existing claims on the capital stock, which is what we mean by the expression "investing in stocks and bonds." The correct response is b.

2.3

Which of the following is the reason why, in the national income accounts, total expenditure for final goods and services is equal to total output?

a. What is produced must be sold.
b. Total expenditure is defined to exclude depreciation.
c. Total expenditure is defined to include the accumulation of inventories.
d. Total expenditure does not include transfer payments.

It is not true that in any time period what is produced must be sold. Consequently, a is not the correct response. The part of output not sold takes the form of an addition to the stock of inventories. In the national income accounts, any accumulation of inventories is counted as an expenditure for final output. The treatment of depreciation and transfer payments in the national income accounts is irrelevant to the question. The correct response is c.

2.4

Which of the following is the reason why, in the national income accounts, total income is equal to total expenditure for final goods and services?

a. *Profit* is defined as the difference between receipts and costs.
b. People spend all that they earn.
c. Indirect business taxes are adjusted to make up any difference.
d. The value-added approach avoids double counting.

Total expenditure for final goods and services is equal to the sum of the values added by all producers. For each producer, the receipts from his sales that remain after paying for the intermediate goods used up are equal to his value added. Part of these remaining receipts is paid to the owners of resources hired to help produce the value added. The remainder takes the form of profit. Thus, for each producer, the income payments (including profit) made to owners of resources used to produce value added add up to the amount of the value added. Because value added for the economy as a whole equals total expenditure for final output, it follows that total income is also equal to total expenditure for final output. The correct response is a.

3

Real vs Money GNP

3.1
In Chapter 1, the concept of national output was defined and analyzed. The main conclusion was that GNP (total output) is the _______________ value of _______________ goods and services.

3.2
In Chapter 2, it was shown that GNP can be measured by either the ___________ for final goods and services or the _________________ earned by the resources used to produce the final goods and services.

3.3
One principal reason for trying to measure output is that because output can serve as a guide to the economic _______________ of a nation, it is useful for policy makers to know whether output is high or low, or rising or falling.

Answers

1. market · final
2. expenditure · income
3. welfare

3.4

Measures of the total output of an economy for any particular year have no meaning unless there is something with which they may be compared. For example, suppose you were told that in 1961 Japan's GNP was 17 trillion yen. By itself, this *(would/would not)* give you any information about the level of economic welfare achieved in the Japanese economy.

3.5

If you also knew that in 1960 Japan's GNP was 14 trillion yen, then the figure for 1961 would acquire meaning, for you would then know that Japan's GNP *(increased/decreased)* from 1960 to 1961. Similarly, if you knew that in 1961 GNP in the United States was 187 trillion yen, the figure for Japan's GNP would tell you that Japan's annual output was substantially *(larger/smaller)* than that of the United States.

3.6

Thus, aggregate measures of economic activity *(do/do not)* indicate the *absolute* level of economic welfare, but *(do/do not)* provide information about *relative* levels of economic welfare.

3.7

In other words, measures of total output of an economy for a particular year are *(not useful/only useful)* for making comparisons. As in the example of Japan's GNP, a measure of total output for a given country in a given year may be compared with the same kind of measure for a different ______________ or a different ______________. Taken by itself, Japan's GNP in 1961 *(is/is not)* a meaningful figure.

3.8

Because changes in a nation's output are of great importance to the well-being of its people, GNP is frequently used to make comparisons over time. And, because it is so important, the major portion of this book is concerned with the

Answers

4. would not
5. increased · smaller
6. do not · do
7. only useful · year · country (either order) · is not

analysis of those factors that lead to changes in GNP over ______________. That is, most of the following chapters will be devoted to the consideration of changes in ______________ for the United States.

3.9

The use of GNP (or similar measures of output) to make comparisons over time involves a number of ambiguities that result from the fact that GNP is a measure of the market ______________ of final goods and services produced. This market value is obtained by using the ______________ of each commodity to measure the relative importance of a unit of each commodity to consumers.

3.10

The price of a commodity is the amount of *money* that must be given up to obtain one unit of the commodity. If stones were used as money, then the price of an automobile would be the number of ______________ that must be paid to obtain the automobile.

3.11

In some economies, stones have been used as money. In others, like prisoner of war camps, cigarettes have been used as money. In the United States, currency issued by the government and other items (such as checks) that can be quickly and cheaply converted into currency are used as ______________.

3.12

The basic monetary unit in the United States is the dollar. Thus, the price of an automobile is the number of ______________ that must be given up to obtain an automobile.

3.13

How are the prices of different commodities determined in a market economy like that of the United States? Consider a typical commodity like overcoats.

Answers

8. time · GNP (output)
9. value · price
10. stones
11. money
12. dollars

Both the consumers who buy and producers who sell overcoats are concerned with the price of overcoats. In general, you would expect that the higher the price of overcoats, the *(more/fewer)* overcoats consumers would be willing to buy and the *(more/fewer)* overcoats producers would be willing to produce and sell.

3.14

Suppose that next year consumers' incomes and preferences and the prices of other commodities are such that they would be willing to buy, or *demand,* the quantity of overcoats for each possible price given below:

Price	*Quantity Demanded*
$150	12 million
200	10 million
250	8 million
300	6 million

This demand schedule shows that the higher the price of overcoats the *(greater/smaller)* will be the quantity demanded.

3.15

Suppose, too, that producers would be willing to sell, or *supply*, the quantities given below:

Price	*Quantity Supplied*
$150	6 million
200	7 million
250	8 million
300	9 million

This supply schedule shows that the higher the price the *(greater/smaller)* will be the quantity supplied.

Answers

13. fewer · more
14. smaller
15. greater

3.16

Suppose that initially the price were to be $200. From the above demand and supply schedules, you know that at a price of $200 consumers will demand

________________ million overcoats but producers will be willing to supply

only ________________ million. At that price, the quantity ________________

will exceed the quantity ________________, and many consumers who are willing to buy overcoats will be unable to do so.

3.17

In this situation, many consumers who otherwise might not get an overcoat will be willing to offer a higher price. Others will not. Because at a price of $200 producers find more customers than they are willing to satisfy at that price, they will be happy to *(raise/lower)* the price.

3.18

In fact, as long as the quantity demanded exceeds the quantity supplied, competition among consumers and the natural willingness of producers to accept a *(higher/lower)* price will result in a *(rise/fall)* in price.

3.19

In the overcoat example, then, as can be seen in the demand and supply schedules shown again below, as long as the price is less than $ ________________ it will tend to rise.

Price	*Quantity Demanded*	*Quantity Supplied*
$150	12 million	6 million
200	10 million	7 million
250	8 million	8 million
300	6 million	9 million

Answers

16. 10 · 7 demanded · supplied
17. raise
18. higher · rise
19. 250

3.20

What if the initial price were to be $300? At that price, the quantity ________ would exceed the quantity ______________. In other words, producers would find themselves producing more overcoats than they could sell.

3.21

In this situation, the more-efficient producers would be able to sell at a lower price and still make a profit. In order to sell their overcoats, these producers would lower their price and thereby induce consumers to buy *(more/fewer)* overcoats and force less-efficient producers to stop producing overcoats.

3.22

Under competitive conditions, as long as quantity supplied is *(greater/smaller)* than quantity demanded, the competition among producers will lead to a decrease in the ______________.

3.23

Thus, as long as the price is more than $ ______________, it will tend to fall.

3.24

Only at a price of $ ______________ will there be no tendency for the price of change because at that price the quantities supplied and demanded will be equal.

3.25

In this example, then, it can be expected that the price of overcoats next year will adjust to a level of $ ______________.

3.26

In general, if markets function properly, the prices of different commodities will move to where the quantities ______________ and ______________ are equal.

Answers

20. supplied · demanded
21. more
22. greater · price
23. 250
24. 250
25. 250
26. supplied · demanded (either order)

3.27

For a fuller understanding of how markets function and how prices are determined in a market economy like the United States, it would be necessary to study microeconomics. This would reveal that consumers help determine the prices of different commodities by the way they spend their income. The preferences of consumers will be reflected in the *(demand/supply)* schedules for different commodities. And, as indicated in Chapter 1, the prices that are determined in free markets will reflect the relative values placed on those commodities by *(consumers/producers)*.

3.28

It is because prices reflect the relative values placed on different commodities by consumers that the market value of all commodities produced, which is ________________, is used as a measure of total output. That is, in using ________________ as a measure of total output the importance or weight given to a unit of any commodity is determined by its ________________.

3.29

Because the prices of different commodities are determined in part by the demand schedules of consumers, and because the quantities supplied by producers depend on prices, it is clear that consumers *(have/do not have)* an important influence on the amounts of different commodities produced. If firms produced commodities that no one would buy at a positive price, they *(would/would not)* be able to sell them at a positive price and *(would/would not)* be able to earn a profit.

3.30

Because businesses are motivated by the desire for profit, in a competitive market economy they will tend to produce commodities in accordance with the preferences of ________________ as reflected in the way ________________ spend their ________________.

Answers

27. demand · consumers
28. GNP · GNP · price
29. have · would not · would not
30. consumers · consumers · income

3.31
What you need to know about microeconomics, then, to help you understand macroeconomics can be summarized as follows:

a. If competitive conditions prevail in markets, as was assumed in the example of the market for overcoats, if the quantity demanded is greater than the quantity supplied, prices will tend to *(rise/fall)* ______. That is, when there is excess demand ______ tend to ______.
b. Conversely, if there is excess supply, ______ will tend to ______.
c. Only when the quantities supplied and demanded are equal will there be no tendency for ______ to change.
d. In competitive markets, the prices that prevail will reflect the relative ______ placed on commodities by consumers, and the quantities produced will be in accordance with the preferences of ______.

3.32
As preferences and incomes change over time, the ______ schedules for different commodities will change. Think, for example, of the demand schedule for Beatles records in 1966 compared with 1956. When demand schedules change, ______ can be expected to change.

3.33
Similarly, as the costs of producing different goods change, their ______ schedules will change. Think, for example, of the supply schedule of radios before and after the invention of the transistor. When supply schedules change, ______ can be expected to change.

3.34
Because the supply and demand schedules for different commodities can be expected to shift in different ways, it can also be expected that ______ of different commodities will not all change in the same way.

Answers

31. a. rise · prices · rise
    b. prices · fall
    c. prices
    d. values · consumers
32. demand · prices
33. supply · prices
34. prices

3.35

Because all prices ___(do/do not)___ change in the same amount, or even in the same direction, in order to determine the general movement in prices it is necessary to find for each period the *average price level.*

3.36

For example, suppose there were just two commodities—meat and Halloween masks—and that last year the price of meat was \$1.00 per pound and the price of a mask was \$1.00. Suppose that this year the price of meat is \$1.10 and the price of masks is 90 cents. What can be said about the general movement of prices? You know that last year the average of the two prices, or the average

______________ ______________, was \$ ______________ .

3.37

It is not so clear, however, what this year's average price level is. At first you might think that it would be a simple average of the two prices, which would be $\frac{\$1.10 + \$0.90}{2}$, or \$ ______________ . But what if many pounds of meat and only a few masks are sold each year? Then the increase in the price of meat is ___(more/less)___ important than the decrease in the price of masks.

3.38

That is, if more pounds of meat than number of masks are sold each year, then you would have to say that in this example the average price level ___(rose/fell)___ from last year to this year.

3.39

To calculate the average price level by using a simple average of individual prices assumes that each commodity ___(is/is not)___ equally important. Because this is not true, it is necessary to count the price of each commodity ___(more/less)___ heavily, the more important that commodity is in the economy.

Answers

35. do not
36. price level · 1.00
37. 1.00 · more
38. rose
39. is · more

3.40

Measures of the average price level are called *price indexes.* There are several different price indexes that are widely used in the United States that measure the ______________ ______________ levels for different groups of commodities. For example, the consumer price ______________ measures the average price level for the goods and services consumers buy. The wholesale ______________ ______________ measures the average price level of goods sold in wholesale trade.

3.41

The price index for any group of commodities is an average of the ______________ of the individual commodities in that group. The more important any commodity is, the *(more/less)* influence will its price have on the index. A small price increase of a very important commodity and a large price increase of an unimportant one *(can/cannot)* result in an increase in the price index.

3.42

Changes in the average price level become important when you want to compare total output for different years. Suppose you want to compare total output in the United States for the two years 1960 and 1968. To do this, you would want to find out what GNP was in each of these years. GNP, of course, is the market value of total ______________, and it can be measured either by total ______________ for final goods and services or total ______________ paid, including depreciation, plus indirect business taxes.

3.43

By looking in the statistical tables in the *Economic Report of the President, 1973,* for example, you will find that GNP increased from $560 billion in 1962 to $1,152 billion in 1972—an increase of 7½ percent per year. If the average price level remained unchanged over this period, then it would be clear that the 7½ percent per year increase in GNP was all due to an increase in the *(prices/production)* of final goods and services.

Answers

40. average price · index · price index
41. prices · more · can
42. output · expenditure · income
43. production

3.44

But suppose that between 1962 and 1972 the average price level rose by 7½ percent per year while production remained unchanged. With this price increase, the market value of output, or GNP, would have *(increased/remained the same)* ________ even though there was no increase in production.

3.45

This example shows that if one knew that GNP rose from 1962 to 1972 by 7½ percent per year, one *(could/could not)* ________ be sure that there was an increase in output. All that one would know is that the ________ value of output increased by 7½ percent per year.

3.46

One way to determine how much of the increase in GNP was due to an increase in real output would be to find out by how much the average ________ ________ increased. If the average price level did not increase at all, then it would be true that *(all/none)* ________ of the 7½ percent per year increase in GNP was due to an increase in production. If the average price level increased by 5½ percent per year, then the increase in GNP due to increased production would be only ________ percent per year.

3.47

In this example, what would it mean if all the increase in GNP was due to an increase in prices? Would it mean that consumers obtained greater satisfaction from the output produced in 1972 than in 1962? Although it is possible that consumers *might* derive more satisfaction from the same quantity of goods and services in one year than in another, the fact that the prices of these commodities rose would not *imply* that this was true. That is, the increase in GNP due merely to an increase in prices *(does/does not)* ________ indicate an increase in economic welfare.

Answers

44. increased
45. could not · market
46. price level · all · 2
47. does not

3.48

An increase in GNP due to an increase in prices indicates only that output produced is sold for more dollars now than before. It does not indicate an increase in ________________ ________________. If it is assumed that consumers' tastes and preferences remain unchanged, it means only that the value of money has *(increased/decreased)* because it now takes more dollars to obtain the same quantity of goods and services.

3.49

The reason for considering price increases as a decrease in the value of ________ rather than as an increase in the real value of output is that goods and services, not money, satisfy consumers' wants. Since consumer satisfaction cannot be measured directly, it is necessary to be content with a measure of output as a guide to economic welfare. As a result, increases in economic welfare are assumed to result from increases in real ________________, but not from increases in ________________.

3.50

If you were to look up the official GNP figures for the United States, you would find that GNP is shown in two ways. One way, which is GNP in *current prices*, is simply GNP as it has been described so far in this book. The other, which is GNP in *constant prices,* is adjusted to eliminate the effects of ________________ changes and to provide a basis for finding the changes in real ________________.

3.51

GNP in constant prices is output valued in terms of the prices in some particular year (the *base* year). For example, GNP for 1962 in 1958 prices is simply the market value of the output produced in 1962 valued in terms of the ____________ that existed in 1958. For the year 1962, GNP valued in terms of 1962 prices is GNP in ________________ prices.

Answers

48. economic welfare · decreased
49. money · output (production) · prices
50. price · output
51. prices · current

3.52

Similarly, GNP for 1972 in 1958 prices is the market value of the output produced in ______________ valued in terms of ______________ prices. For 1972, GNP in 1972 prices is GNP in ______________ prices.

3.53

Any price changes that occurred between 1962 and 1972 will not influence the change in output as measured by GNP in ______________ ______________, because each year's output is valued in terms of *(the same/different)* ______ prices.

3.54

Earlier it was noted that GNP in current prices increased by 7½ percent per year from 1962 to 1972. Over the same period, GNP in 1958 prices increased by slightly more than 4 percent per year. In other words, over this ten-year period the annual real output increased by slightly more than ______________ percent per year, and the price level increased by nearly ______________ percent per year.

3.55

To emphasize the difference between these two GNP concepts, GNP in current prices is frequently called *money* GNP, and GNP in constant prices is frequently called *real* GNP. The term *money GNP* emphasizes that GNP in ______________ prices measures the annual money expenditure. The term *real GNP* emphasizes that GNP in ______________ prices measures increases in the annual production of goods and services.

3.56

The reason money GNP and real GNP can change in different ways is that, even when there are no changes in the production of output, changes in money expenditure for output can reflect changes in ______________.

Answers

52. 1972 · 1958 · current
53. constant prices (1958 prices) · the same
54. 4 · 3½
55. current · constant
56. prices

3.57

It should be emphasized that prices play an important role in the construction of both money and real GNP. Both GNP measures use the prices of different commodities to determine the relative importance of units of those commodities. If commodity A has a low price and commodity B a high price, then a unit of A makes up a relatively *(small/large)* part of total output and a unit of B makes up a relatively *(small/large)* part of total output.

3.58

The only difference between money GNP and real GNP is that each uses a different set of ______________ to value output for any year. For the output of 1970, for example, money GNP uses the prices for ______________, whereas real GNP uses the prices for some ______________ year.

3.59

The reason money GNP should not be used for making comparisons of output over time is that it is affected by both ______________ and ______________ changes. By using real GNP, a change in GNP will reflect only changes in ______________.

3.60

Figure 3.1 indicates the quantitative importance of the distinction between money and real GNP. Because 1958 was chosen as the base year in Figure 3.1, money and real GNP are ______________ in that year.

3.61

The fact that money GNP lies *(above/below)* real GNP before 1958 and *(above/below)* after 1958 indicates that there has been a general *(upward/downward)* trend in the average price level.

Answers

57. small · large
58. prices · 1970 · base
59. output · price (either order) · output
60. equal
61. below · above · upward

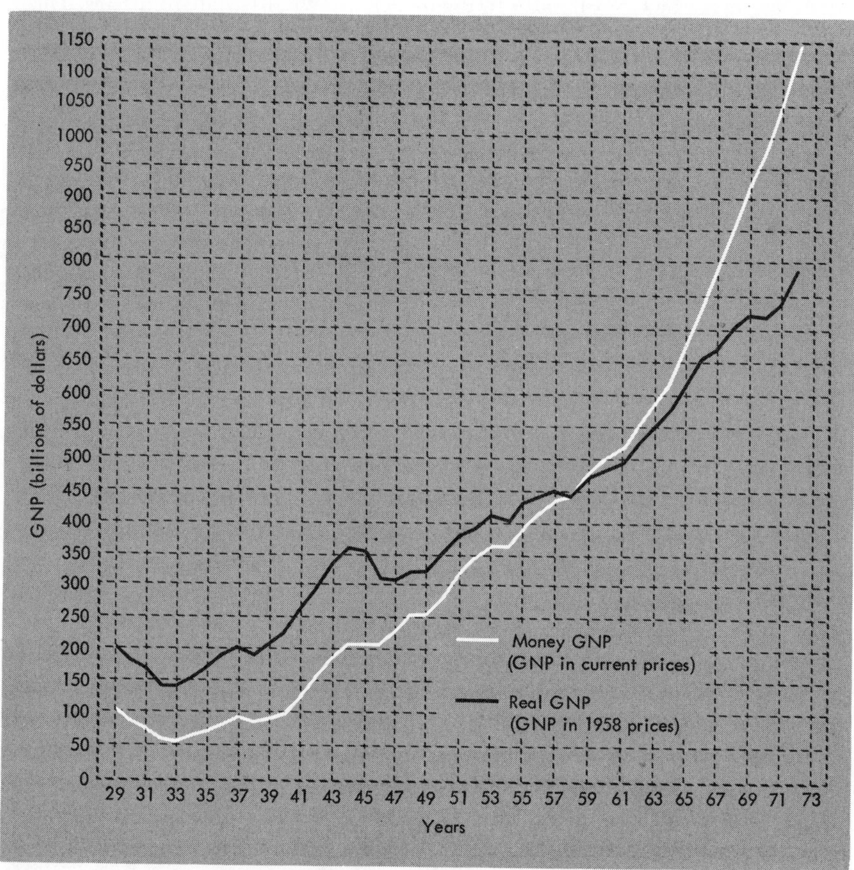

FIGURE 3.1 Money and Real GNP, 1929–1972

3.62

In practice, real GNP is obtained by dividing money GNP by a price index for all final goods and services. This index, which is called the GNP *deflator,* measures the average ________________ ________________ of all final goods and services. The GNP deflator is shown in Figure 3.2. Because 1958 is the base year, the GNP ________________ for 1958 has a value of 1.00.

Answers

62. price level · deflator

3.63

In other years, the GNP deflator in Figure 3.2 will be different from 1.00. This difference is due to the fact that the average ______________ level was different in those years from the 1958 level. For example, as shown in Figure 3.2, the value for 1972 was about ______________. This means that the average price level in 1972 was about ______________ percent higher than the 1958 level.

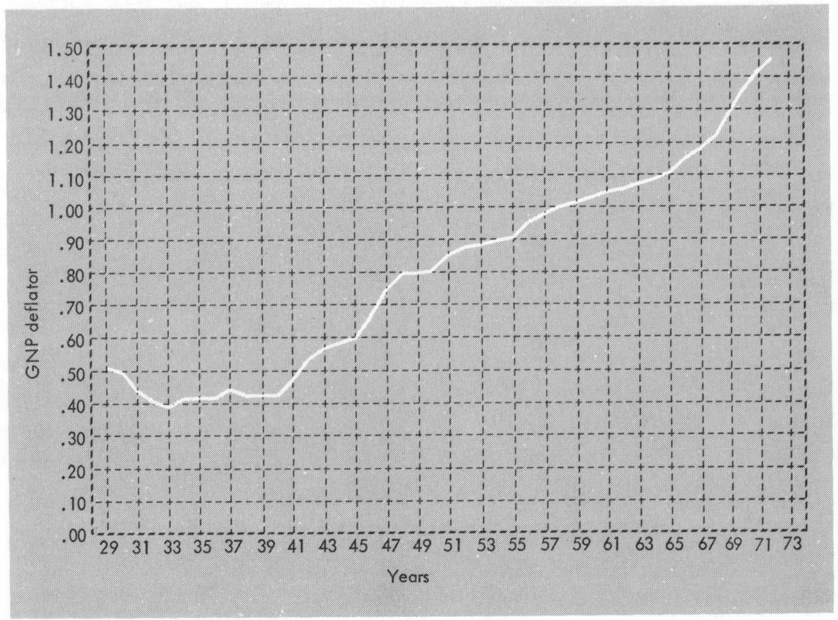

FIGURE 3.2 GNP Deflator, 1929–1972 (1958 = 1.00)

3.64

The GNP ______________ is a price ______________. It shows how the price level in any year compares with the price level in the ______________ year.

Answers

63. price · 1.46 · 46
64. deflator · index · base

3.65

An increase in the price level is called *inflation.* Similarly, a decrease in the price level is termed *deflation.* The GNP deflator in Figure 3.2 has *(increased/decreased)* almost every year since 1933. As a result, one would conclude from this information that nearly the entire period was one of ______________ .

3.66

Although practically all economists would agree that over this period there have been many years of inflation, many economists argue that the changes in the GNP deflator are *biased* upwards. By this they mean that the GNP deflator tends to *(overstate/understate)* the amount of inflation in the economy. That is, they believe that when, in fact, there is average price stability the GNP deflator is likely to *(increase/decrease)* .

3.67

What reason is there to think that the GNP deflator shows more ______________ than there really is? Consider the case of one commodity: film.

3.68

Suppose that the price of film had remained constant from 1929 to 1972. Would the buyer of film in 1929 or in 1972 have obtained more for his money? Because the quality of film has increased substantially over this period—for example, film is now available in color and is both faster and more light sensitive—you would have to say that the *(1929/1972)* film would be a better buy.

3.69

In fact, the price of film has risen since 1929. But because the ______________ of film has also increased over this period, it is not clear that, even though the price has increased, you would not get more for your money buying film in 1972 than you could have in 1929.

Answers

65. increased · inflation
66. overstate · increase
67. inflation
68. 1972
69. quality

3.70

If the quality increase just matched the price increase, then it would be possible to conclude that if film were the only commodity, there ___*(was/was no)*___ inflation.

3.71

The actual increase in the price of a commodity would provide an accurate measure of the real price increase only if the nature of the commodity ___*(remained the same/changed)*___ . If the quality of a commodity increases, then the actual price increase will be ___*(greater/smaller)*___ than the real price increase.

3.72

When one considers the range of commodities for which substantial increases in quality have occurred, the importance of this problem becomes apparent. Despite the familiar saying that "they don't make things the way they used to," it is clear that the improvements in the ______________ of such different commodities as automobiles and medical services, typewriters and clothing, records and the packaging and processing of food make it difficult to identify the true rate of ______________ from the GNP deflator.

3.73

Because it is practically impossible to measure the improvements in quality of most commodities, it is necessary, in the construction of a price index, to ignore a large portion of quality change. It is for this reason that many economists consider changes in the GNP deflator to be biased ______________ .

3.74

Although no one has any firm basis for making such a judgment, many economists consider about a 2 percent per year increase in the GNP deflator to be "true" price stability. This would be correct if the average annual improvement in ______________ were in this range.

Answers

70. was no
71. remained the same · greater
72. quality · inflation
73. upward
74. quality

3.75

If one were to accept this judgment, then the earlier conclusion that practically the whole period since 1933 was marked by _______________ no longer holds true. This earlier conclusion was based on the fact that the GNP deflator *(increased/decreased)* throughout most of this period.

3.76

The information in Figure 3.2 has been used in a different way in Figure 3.3. Figure 3.2 shows the *(level of/change in)* the GNP deflator for the years given along the horizontal axis. From this, it is possible to calculate for each year the percentage change in the GNP deflator, which is called the rate of inflation. Figure 3.3, then, shows for each year since 1929 the _______________ of _______________.

3.77

A careful examination of Figure 3.3 shows that of the 43 years shown, the rate of inflation was greater than 2 percent in _______________ years and less than 2 percent in _______________ years. Thus, if allowance is made for possible quality improvement of about 2 percent per year, there was no inflation problem in about half the years shown in Figure 3.3.

3.78

Although there were many years when the rate of increase in the GNP deflator did not exceed the _______________ percent judged by many economists to be "true" price stability, for the last 7 years shown in Figure 3.3 the rate of inflation *(was/was not)* greater than 2 percent per year.

3.79

This fact emphasizes the importance of distinguishing between real and money GNP. In years of rapid inflation, the increase in production would have been greatly overstated if reliance were placed solely on _______________ GNP as a measure of output.

Answers

75. inflation · increased
76. level of · rate · inflation
77. 22 · 21
78. 2 · was
79. money

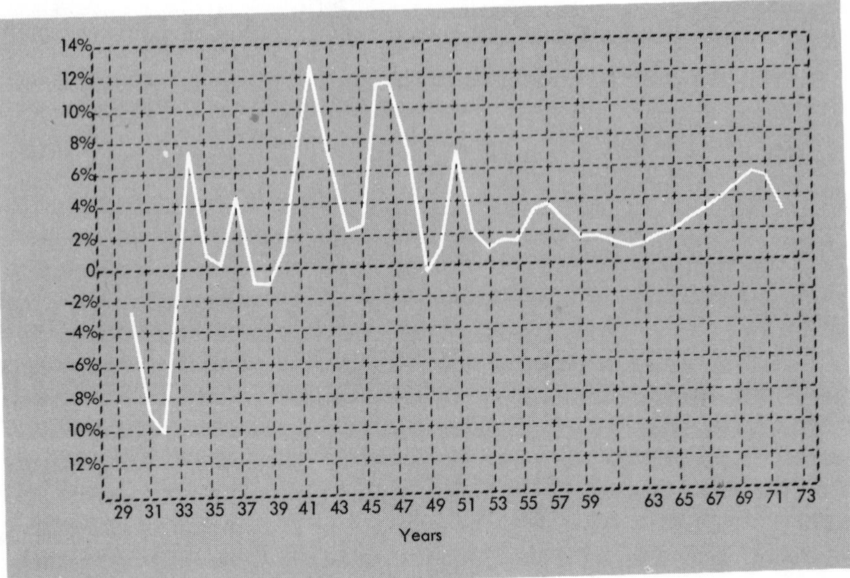

FIGURE 3.3 Change in GNP Deflator, 1930—1972

3.80

In order to make comparisons of output over time that are not distorted by changes in the price level, it is necessary to use ______________ GNP, which is output valued in ______________ prices.

REVIEW QUESTIONS

3.1

If money GNP fell more rapidly than real GNP during some period, which of the following must be true?

a. The average price level must have fallen.
b. The average price level must have fallen more rapidly than production.
c. The average price level must have risen.
d. The average price level must have risen more rapidly than production.

Answers

80. real · constant

Suppose that money GNP fell by 6 percent and real GNP fell by 4 percent; the average price level must have fallen by 2 percent. Because the price level is the ratio of money GNP to real GNP, the only way for money GNP to fall more than real GNP is for the price level to fall. The correct response is a.

3.2

If quality improvements in the goods produced often go unmeasured,

a. it is better to use money rather than real GNP.
b. the rate of inflation must always exceed 2 percent.
c. there is a difference between real and money GNP.
d. the official price indexes tend to indicate more inflation than there really is.

When comparing the price of a good in two time periods, the comparison will have meaning only if the nature of the good in question is the same in the two periods. If the quality of the good has improved or deteriorated over time, then a direct comparison of the prices in the two periods will not provide an accurate indication of how the value of the dollar has changed when used to buy that good. If, as is generally thought to be the case, average unmeasured changes in quality are improvements, then official price indexes will overstate the amount of inflation. If, however, the average change represents a deterioration in quality, then the official price indexes will understate the rate of inflation. The correct response is d.

3.3

Historically, real GNP has risen less rapidly than money GNP. Which of the following does this imply must be true?

1. If there had been less inflation, there would have been more growth in real GNP.
2. The general price level has risen.
3. Price indexes have not reflected improvements in product quality.
   a. 1 and 2 only
   b. 2 only
   c. 2 and 3 only
   d. 1, 2, and 3

By definition, whenever GNP in current prices rose more rapidly than GNP in constant prices, it means that the average price level rose. A rise in the price level does not necessarily come at the expense of a greater rise in real output. If there had been less inflation, the result may simply have meant lower growth in money GNP. Also, it is possible to have price increases when there are no unmeasured quality improvements. Thus far in this book, we have not analyzed the causes or the consequences of inflation; we have simply worked understanding what inflation is. The correct response is b.

3.4

An economy producing just cards and curds had a record of prices and production as follows:

	First year	*Second year*
Cards		
Output	150	100
Price	$1.00	$2.00
Curds		
Output	700	1000
Price	$ .50	$ .40

Fill in the following table:

	First year	*Second year*
Money GNP	______	______
Real GNP in first year prices	______	______
GNP deflator	______	______

Money GNP is the market value (price times quantity) of all final goods and services produced using current year prices in each year. Money GNP was $500 for the base year and $600 for this year. Real GNP in first-year prices is the market value of output produced using first-year prices to value the output in each year. Because the first year is the base year, real GNP in the first year must be the same as for money GNP, $500. For the second year, real GNP in first-year prices would be 100 X $1.00 plus 1000 X $0.50, or $600. The GNP deflator is the ratio of money GNP to real GNP in each year. In the first year this must be 1.00. For the second year, the ratio is also 1.00, which means there was no inflation between the first year and the second year.

4

Actual vs Potential GNP

4.1

Up to this point, the discussion has centered on the problem of how to measure the output of an economy, but it has not dealt with the question of what determines how much output there will be. Before considering this question, however, the following points should be clear:

a. GNP is the ________________ ________________ of final goods and services produced in a year.

b. It can be measured by either the total ________________ for final goods and services or the total ________________ earned in producing that output.

c. In order to compare GNP for different time periods, it is necessary to use ________________ GNP, which excludes changes in expenditure and income that result from changes in the ________________ level.

Answers

1. a. market value
   b. expenditure · income
   c. real · price

4.2

Because it is important always to use ______________ GNP when making comparisons over time, whenever the term *GNP* is used in that context in this book it should be understood to mean real GNP. For example, if the statement is made that GNP in 1972 was 6 percent greater than in 1971; it means that ______________ GNP, not ______________ GNP, was 6 percent greater. In reading newspapers reports of changes in GNP, however, it is important to find out which of these concepts is being discussed.

4.3

Real GNP gives a measure of the output actually produced. What real GNP is in any year depends on the quantity of ______________ used in production and how efficiently those ______________ are used.

4.4

Unfortunately, there have been periods when the quantity of resources used has been less than the quantity available. As a result, in those periods real GNP has *(been equal to/fallen below)* the level that could have been obtained if all available resources had been utilized. The level of output that *can* be obtained when resources are fully utilized is called *potential* GNP.

4.5

When actual GNP is equal to potential GNP, the economy's ______________ are fully utilized. When the available resources are fully utilized, actual GNP is equal to ______________ GNP.

4.6

Figure 4.1 shows, for the period 1929–1972, the percentage of those persons willing and able to work who were unemployed. This number is called the *unemployment rate.* The year in which the ______________ rate was highest was ______________. In 1953, the unemployment rate was considerably lower–

Answers

2. real · real · money
3. resources · resources
4. fallen below
5. resources · potential
6. unemployment · 1933

only about _______________ percent as compared to _______________ percent in 1933.

4.7

For an economy like that of the United States, in which there is a great deal of mobility, there will always be resources shifting from one use or location to another. Such reallocation takes time and results in temporary unemployment. If

there are always some resources in the process of shifting, then the __________ rate will never be zero. If you look at Figure 4.1, you will see that for the years shown the unemployment rate *(has/has never)* ______ fallen to zero.

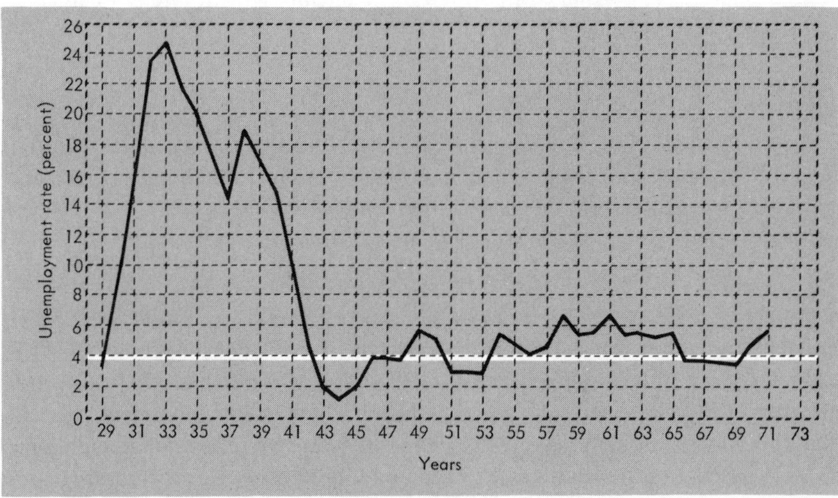

FIGURE 4.1 Unemployment rate, 1929–1972.

4.8

Because unemployment due to the reallocation of resources is considered normal in a free market economy, *full employment* is often defined to exist when the number of workers unemployed is 4 percent of the labor force or less. Thus, it is

clear that in 1953, for example, by this definition there was _______________ employment, and in 1937 there *(also was/was not)* ______ full employment.

Answers

6. 3 · 25
7. unemployment · has never
8. full · was not

4.9

The concepts of *potential GNP* and full employment are tied together. That is, *potential GNP* is defined to mean the output obtainable if there were full employment. Thus, in order for GNP to be equal to potential GNP, it is not necessary for the ______________ rate to be zero. Potential GNP is the output that would be produced if the unemployment rate were ______________ percent or less.

4.10

If you look at Figure 4.1 again, you will see that, for the years 1943–1945, the unemployment rate fell well below 4 percent. That is, even though full ______________ is assumed to prevail if the unemployment rate is 4 percent, it *(is/is not)* impossible to get it even lower.

4.11

It should be made clear, however, that the years in which the unemployment rate fell far below 4 percent were war years, when the normal functioning of markets was disrupted. Aside from this period, there *(were/were no)* years in which the unemployment rate fell as low as 3 percent.

4.12

Full employment is often said to exist when the unemployment rate is ________ percent or less. But, to simplify the discussion, henceforth a period of full employment will be referred to as a period during which there is no unemployment. You should remember, however, that the more clumsy phrase "no unemployment above 4 percent of the labor force" would be *(more/less)* accurate.

4.13

From Figure 4.1, it is clear that there were many years between 1929 and 1971 when the unemployment rate rose above 4 percent. In those years, actual GNP fell below ______________ GNP.

Answers

9. unemployment · 4
10. employment · is not
11. were no
12. 4 · more
13. potential

4.14

Studies have been made to calculate what GNP would have been in those years if there had been 4 percent employment. The result of those calculations, which is ______________ GNP, is shown in Figure 4.2, along with actual GNP, in 1958 prices.

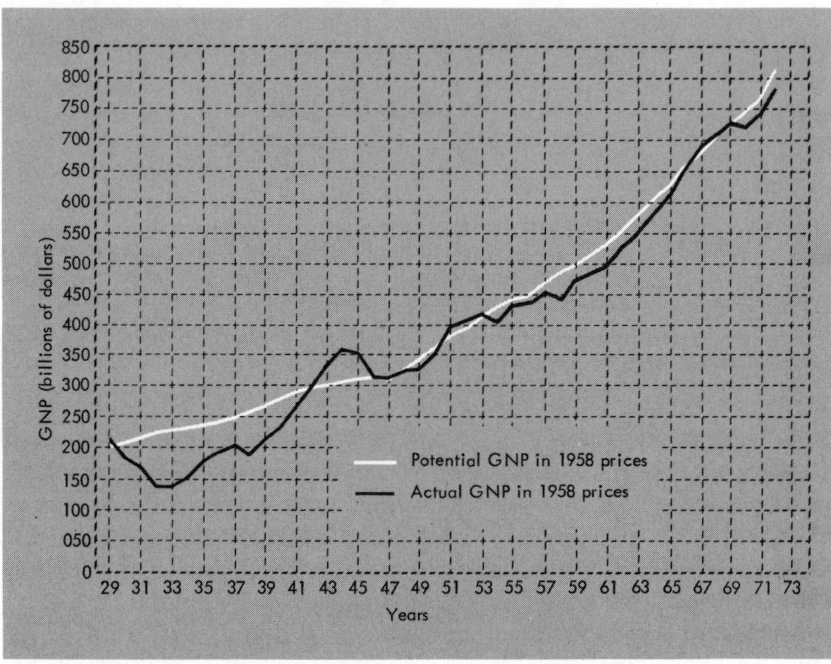

FIGURE 4.2 Actual GNP and potential GNP, 1929–1972 (1958 prices)

4.15

The difference between actual and potential GNP is the ______________ lost when resources are wasted in umemployment. In Figure 4.2, actual GNP appears to be greater than potential GNP. That is a result of measuring potential GNP as the real GNP that would result if unemployment were equal to 4 percent of the labor force. In the years when actual GNP exceeded potential GNP measured in this way, the unemployment rate was less than ______________ percent.

Answers

14. potential
15. output · 4

4.16
To understand how substantial the losses from unemployment can be, consider the following information taken from Figures 4.1 and 4.2 for the year 1961:

	GNP in 1958 prices	*Unemployment rate*
Actual situation	$497 billion	6.7 percent
Full employment situation	$530 billion	4.0 percent

In 1961, the unemployment rate was ______________ percent and real GNP was $ ______________ billion. If the unemployment rate had been 4.0 percent, real GNP would have been $ ______________ billion.

4.17
Thus, in 1961, $ ______________ billion of output was lost because resources were wasted in ______________ . When you know that this loss was greater than the entire GNP of either Australia or Canada in 1961, you realize how great the costs of unemployment can be.

4.18
In 1968, unlike 1961, the economy was at full employment. This means, of course, that in 1968 actual GNP was equal to ______________ ______________.

4.19
In comparing 1961 and 1968, it is helpful to look at the following table:

	1961	*1968*
Unemployment rate	6.7 percent	3.6 percent
Potential GNP (1958 prices)	$530 billion	$707 billion
Actual GNP (1958 prices)	$497 billion	$707 billion
Output gap	$ 33 billion	$ 0 billion

Answers

16. 6.7 · 497 · 530
17. 33 · unemployment
18. potential GNP

Between 1961 and 1968, unemployment fell from _______________ to _______________ percent of the labor force. As a result, the gap between actual and potential GNP was reduced from $ _______________ billion to $ _______________ billion.

4.20
This means that part of the increase in output between 1961 and 1968 resulted from the fact that some of the resources that were _______________ in 1961 were being used to produce output in _______________ .

4.21
Whenever there is above-normal unemployment, resources that could be used to satisfy consumers' _______________ are being wasted in idleness. In 1961, then, it would have been possible to make many consumers better off if the ________ resources could have been put to use.

4.22
Many consider that there is an added cost of high unemployment because the loss of output and income is not borne equally by all groups of society. Those persons who become unemployed suffer *(large/small)* _______ losses of income, but those who continue to work experience little if any loss of _______________ from an increase in the unemployment rate.

4.23
It is interesting to observe how the unemployment rates for different population groups changed as the overall unemployment rate changed between 1961 and 1968. This information is shown in the following table.

Answers

19. 6.7 · 3.6 · 33 · 0
20. unemployed · 1968
21. wants · unemployed
22. large · income

SELECTED UNEMPLOYMENT RATES, 1961, 1968

	1961	*1968*
All workers	6.7	3.6
White	6.0	3.2
Nonwhite	12.4	6.7
White collar	3.3	2.0
Blue collar	9.2	4.1

What these data indicate is that when the overall unemployment rate changes the unemployment rates of different groups change by *(equal/different)* ______ amounts.

4.24

Between 1961 and 1968, the unemployment rate for white workers declined by ______________ percentage points, but for nonwhite workers the decline was ______________ percentage points.

4.25

Similarly, the unemployment rate for white-collar workers declined by ________ percentage points, but for blue-collar workers the decline was ______________ percentage points.

4.26

The general pattern seems to be that when unemployment rises the groups that tend to be hurt most (nonwhite and blue-collar workers) are those with *(above/below)* -average incomes. Also, when unemployment is reduced these same groups benefit *(least/most)* ______.

4.27

Because changes in unemployment tend to affect especially lower-income groups, the persons who are most seriously hurt by high unemployment are those who can *(most/least)* ______ afford the resulting loss of income.

Answers

23. different
24. 2.8 · 5.7
25. 1.3 · 5.1
26. below · most
27. least

4.28

For many people, the consequences of a rise in the overall rate from 3 or 4 percent to 6 or 7 percent means substantial *(gains/losses)* in what are already *(above/below)* average incomes. As a result, high unemployment can only aggravate the already serious problems of hunger, poverty, and crime that plague lower-income groups.

4.29

It is clear that high unemployment is a serious economic problem. It results in a substantial loss of _______________ that could be used to satisfy the wants of _______________. Also, to many this loss is all the more regrettable because the excess unemployment is largely concentrated in *(high/low)* -income groups.

4.30

Unemployment, of course, arises when _______________ GNP is less than _______________ GNP. For this reason, when potential GNP increases actual GNP must also increase to avoid _______________.

4.31

Frequently, increases in unemployment are blamed on factors that cause potential GNP to rise. According to this view, the way to prevent _______________ is to keep _______________ GNP from rising.

4.32

Potential GNP can be thought of as the average GNP per worker times the number of workers in the labor force. If either average _______________ per worker or the size of the _______________ force goes up, potential GNP will go up also.

Answers

28. losses · below
29. output · consumers · low
30. actual · potential · unemployment
31. unemployment · potential
32. GNP · labor

4.33

Average GNP per worker is usually called *labor productivity.* When the output that the average worker can produce goes up, then it is said that there has been an increase in labor _______________ .

4.34

Those who worry about the effect of growth in potential GNP on unemployment are concerned that existing workers will no longer be needed when labor _______________ increases; or that new workers will not find jobs when the labor _______________ increases.

4.35

For this worry to be justified, there must be a reason why actual GNP cannot keep pace with potential GNP. As long as it is possible to increase actual GNP, the best way to prevent unemployment is not to keep _______________ GNP from increasing but to make sure that _______________ GNP expands along with _______________ GNP. In this way, it will be possible to avoid _________ and still have an increasing _______________ .

4.36

Over past decades in the United States, there has been substantial growth in both labor productivity and the labor force. That is, growth in potential GNP has resulted from an increase in both average _______________ per _______________ and the number of _______________ .

4.37

Figure 4.3 shows the growth in labor productivity since 1929. Throughout most of this period, average GNP per worker has *(increased/decreased)* so that in 1972 labor _______________ was about *(2/3/4)* times higher than in 1929. This amounts to an average increase of nearly 2 percent per year.

Answers

33. productivity
34. productivity · force
35. potential · actual · potential · unemployment · GNP
36. GNP · worker · workers
37. increased · productivity · 2

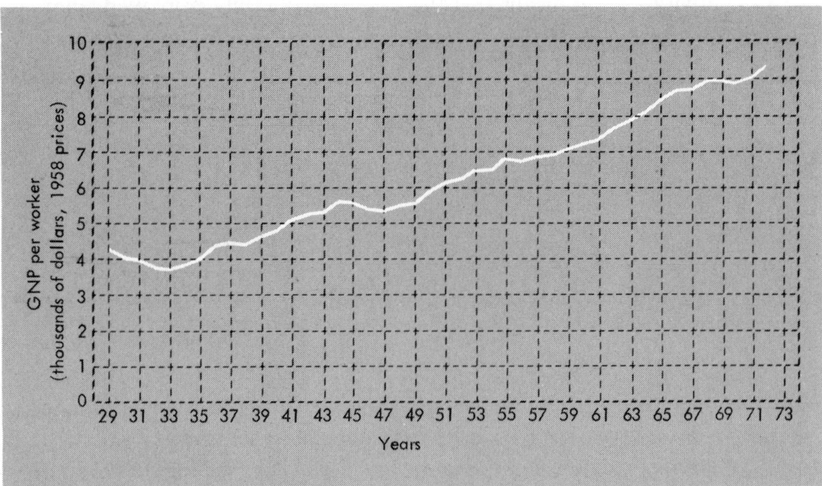

FIGURE 4.3 GNP per worker, 1929–1972 (1958 prices)

4.38

Given the approximate doubling of labor ______________ between 1929 and 1972, it would be possible to produce in 1972 the same GNP as in 1929 with only about ______________ as many workers. Over this period, however, the number of available workers increased by 80 percent.

4.39

As a result, if output had not increased between 1929 and 1972, there would have been a very high rate of ______________ in 1972—on the order of 70 percent. From Figure 4.1, which showed unemployment rates for this time period, it is clear that the unemployment rate in 1972 *(was/was not)* higher than in 1929, *(nearly/but not nearly)* as high as 70 percent.

4.40

This means that increases in productivity between 1929 and 1972 have not forced the economy to accept a higher rate of ______________ but have made possible a higher level of ______________ .

Answers

38. productivity · half
39. unemployment · was · but not nearly
40. unemployment · GNP

4.41

These same ideas can be expressed in terms of potential and actual GNP. When labor productivity rises, it means that the output that a fully employed labor force could produce *(rises/falls)* ________ . That is, when labor productivity goes up, given the size of the labor force, ________ GNP increases.

4.42

If actual GNP fails to keep pace with potential GNP, then the productivity change results in ________ . But if actual GNP does remain equal to potential GNP, then ________ change leads to higher levels of income and expenditure.

4.43

Even though there have been periods of high unemployment, the fact that actual GNP has repeatedly caught up with potential GNP (see Figure 4.2) indicates that productivity increases need not be wasted in high ________ but can result in higher ________, as well as potential, GNP.

4.44

The labor force also grew throughout the 1929–1972 period. In 1972, there were over 89 million workers compared to less than 50 million in 1929. This represents an average annual increase of about 1¼ percent. Even if labor productivity had remained constant, there would have had to be an average yearly increase in GNP of ________ percent to prevent ________ from rising over the period.

4.45

Because potential GNP equals labor productivity times the number of workers in the labor force, the rate of growth in potential GNP is approximately equal to the rate of increase in labor ________ *plus* the rate of increase in the labor ________ .

Answers

41. rises · potential
42. unemployment · productivity
43. unemployment · actual
44. 1¼ · unemployment
45. productivity · force (either order)

4.46

Since 1929, growth in labor productivity has averaged 2 percent per year, and growth in the labor force has averaged 1¼ percent per year. Consequently, potential GNP has grown at an average rate of ______________ percent per year. Also, because actual and potential were equal both in 1929 and 1968, the average rate of growth of actual GNP during that period must have been ______________ percent per year. Since 1968, however, actual GNP has grown *(faster/slower)* than potential GNP, and the unemployment rate has *(risen above/fallen below)* 4 percent.

4.47

It is clear that labor force growth is the result of population growth. But what is it that causes growth in labor productivity? One factor is the education and skill of the labor force. The better educated and more highly trained workers are, the higher will be their ______________ .

4.48

Education and skill are sometimes referred to as *human capital.* Just like capital goods (machinery and so on), human ______________ can be increased by investment. By devoting output to education and training, it is possible to give workers more ______________ ______________ and thereby increase their ______________ .

4.49

A second factor that has led to higher labor productivity has been the growth in the amount of capital goods. The more capital goods the average worker has to use, the more ______________ he can produce, and the greater will be his ______________ .

4.50

The quantity of capital goods has increased over time as a result of ______________ expenditure by businesses.

Answers

46. 3¼ · 3¼ · slower · risen above
47. productivity
48. capital · human capital · productivity
49. output · productivity
50. investment

4.51

A third factor that has raised labor productivity has been *technical progress,* which is an improvement in the technological and organizational know-how relating to production. The invention of the transistor and the adoption of mass production are examples of ______________ progress that increased labor ______________ .

4.52

For any particular period of time, an economy's potential GNP will have been determined by past events. For this year, to take an example, the labor force in the United States has been determined by *(present/past)* population growth. This year's births can add to the labor force only in the *(present/future)* .

4.53

Similarly, the level of labor productivity will have been influenced by past ______________ for education and training, plant and equipment, and research and development. But expenditure for these items in the present will only have an effect on future labor ______________ .

4.54

It is possible for events that take place in the current period to affect the potential GNP of future periods. But for the current period, potential GNP can be regarded as having been already determined. That is, in the *long* run, when allowance is made for the passage of time and the accompanying technological progress and growth in the quantity of resources, potential GNP can be considered to be *(fixed/variable)* . But, in the *short* run, when the sole consideration is what occurs in the present period of time, potential GNP can be taken to be *(fixed/variable)* .

4.55

In the short run, there is a limit to the level of GNP. For any normal period, ______________ GNP cannot exceed ______________ GNP. Because in the

Answers

51. technical · productivity
52. past · future
53. expenditure · productivity
54. variable · fixed
55. actual · potential

short run potential GNP is _______________ , the main policy issue concerns the gap between actual and potential.

4.56

In the long run, there is no ceiling on GNP. By investing in education, capital goods, and research, it is possible to increase labor _______________ and, thereby, _______________ GNP. As a result, in the long run the main interest of policy shifts to the question of whether the economy is investing enough to increase _______________ GNP at a fast enough rate.

4.57

In the following chapters, the main topic for discussion will be short-run policy. Two questions to be answered are: Why does _______________ GNP sometimes fall short of _______________ GNP? And, what happens when there is an attempt to raise actual _______________ above potential _______________ ?

REVIEW QUESTIONS

4.1

During a period of no technological change, it was observed that real GNP expanded at a faster rate than potential GNP. Comparing the beginning of this period with the end of the period, it can be concluded that

a. the economy was operating at full employment at the end of the period.
b. the economy was operating at less than full employment at the beginning of the period.
c. the labor force was increasing throughout the period.
d. the labor force was decreasing throughout the period.

If the economy were at full employment at the beginning of the period, the maximum rate of growth of real GNP would be determined by the rate of growth of potential GNP. This would be true independent of any changes in

Answers

55. fixed
56. productivity · potential · potential
57. actual · potential · GNP · GNP

the size of the labor force. Consequently, for real GNP to grow faster than potential GNP means that the economy initially was at less than full employment. The correct response is b.

4.2

If the labor force and labor productivity both increase, then:

a. real GNP will increase.
b. unemployment will increase.
c. either a or b, or both.
d. None of the above is correct.

An increase in both the labor force and labor productivity will increase potential GNP. Thus, it is possible for real GNP to increase. But because it is possible for actual GNP to fall below potential GNP, real GNP will not necessarily increase. If real GNP failed to increase, unemployment would increase. It is possible, however, that real GNP would increase but not by as much as potential GNP, in which case unemployment would also increase. Either real GNP or unemployment or both must increase. The correct response is c.

4.3

Which, if any, of the following would be a possible consequence of adopting technological innovations that resulted in higher output per worker?

1. Lower employment
2. Higher national output
   a. 1 only
   b. 2 only
   c. both 1 and 2
   d. neither 1 nor 2

If higher national output did not result, an increase in output per worker would be accompanied by a reduction in the number of workers employed and/or a reduction in average hours worked per week. If lower employment did not result, higher output per worker would lend to higher national output. Consequently, both 1 and 2 are possible. Of course, it is also possible with a productivity increase to have simultaneously lower employment and higher national output. The correct response is c.

4.4

The following data, *in index form,* refer to a hypothetical economy:

	Real GNP	*Money GNP*	*Potential GNP*	*Labor Force*
1972	100	100	100	100
1973	104	106	100	103

Which of the following can be inferred from the above data?

1. Labor productivity decreased between 1972 and 1973.
2. Prices rose on average by about 2 percent between 1972 and 1973.
   a. 1 only
   b. 2 only
   c. both 1 and 2
   d. neither 1 nor 2

Because the labor force increased and potential GNP did not change, the labor productivity must have decreased. If productivity had remained constant, potential GNP would have changed due to the increase in the labor force. Money GNP increased by 2 percent more than real GNP. This difference was due to a rise in the price level by this amount. The correct response is c.

5

Aggregate Demand and Supply

5.1
The annual output of the U.S. economy has grown substantially in past years. This has been made possible by increases in ________ output.

5.2
But at times, this growth has been accompanied by large increases in the price level. That is, there have been periods of time when the economy faced the problem of ________.

5.3
At other times, annual output actually decreased, or failed to increase as rapidly as possible. In those periods, output fell below ________ output as resources became ________.

Answers

1. potential
2. inflation
3. potential · unemployed

5.4

What are the causes of inflation and unemployment? Why is it that in some periods ______ tend to rise and in others ______ become unemployed? To answer these important questions, it is useful to introduce a simply *model* of the economy. A model states relationships among a number of economic variables, such as GNP, the average price level, and so on. In order to be useful, the relationships stated in a ______ must be a reasonably close approximation to the aspect of the actual economy under study.

5.5

At the same time, however, the model must be simple enough to facilitate the understanding of the actual economy. That is, a ______ of the economy must *(retain/exclude)* the essential features of the economy in order to be realistic and must *(retain/exclude)* the unnecessary details of the real world in order to be simple enough to understand easily.

5.6

Models are important to economists because they enable the economist to isolate and concentrate on the *(more/less)* important variables and relationships in the economy.

5.7

As a model is developed, the simplifying assumptions will be made explicit so that it is clear how it differs from the real world. But even though the model *(will/will not)* be an exact replica of the real world, it can help answer the questions that have been asked about inflation and ______.

5.8

Because the United States has a market economy, the quantity of output that firms are willing to produce and the price at which they can sell their output depend on the total ______ for output that consumers, businesses, and governments are willing to make at different price levels.

Answers

4. prices · resources · model
5. model · retain · exclude
6. more
7. will not · unemployment
8. expenditure

5.9

As you learned in Chapter 2, total dollar expenditure must be equal to money GNP. A change in total dollar expenditure must be accompanied by a change in ______ GNP. But, as you learned in Chapter 3, a change in total expenditure *(must/need not)* be accompanied by a change in real GNP.

5.10

For example, if total expenditure increases by 5 percent, then ______ GNP must increase by 5 percent. If the price level remains the same, then ______ GNP must also increase by 5 percent. But if the price level increases by 5 percent, real GNP will increase by *(0/5)* percent.

5.11

Thus, an increase in total expenditure will always result in an increase in ______ GNP, but may or may not result in an increase in ______ GNP.

5.12

In order to understand when an increase in total expenditure will be accompanied by an increase in real GNP and when by an increase in the price level, it is useful to think in terms of the total expenditure that would be made *if prices were to remain unchanged.* This is called *aggregate demand.* Although very simple, this concept is very important, so be sure you know its definition. The total expenditure that would be made if ______ were to remain ______ is called aggregate ______.

5.13

Sometimes economists use the term *aggregate demand* to mean total spending regardless of the level of prices. But here, because it makes the analysis clearer, what we mean by aggregate demand is the total ______ that would result with a *(given/changing)* price level.

Answers

9. money · need not
10. money · real · 0
11. money · real
12. prices · unchanged · demand
13. expenditure · given

5.14

What will be the effect of a change in aggregate demand on the price level and on real GNP? Suppose the economy were initially at full employment. Then, of course, actual GNP would initially be equal to ________ GNP. Now suppose there were an increase in aggregate demand. This means that if the price level were to remain unchanged, consumers, businesses, and governments taken together would be willing to purchase *(more/less)* output than before.

5.15

Because the economy was initially at full employment, it *(would/would not)* be possible for producers to increase production because there *(would/would not)* be unemployed resources available.

5.16

Thus, the increase in aggregate demand means that, at initial prices, buyers would be trying to buy *(more/less)* output than could be produced. In such a situation, competition among buyers would tend to drive the price level *(up/down)* .

5.17

What this example makes clear is that when aggregate demand exceeds potential GNP valued in initial prices, the price level will *(increase/decrease)* . Thus, according to our model, inflation will result whenever the level of ________ ________ is greater than ________ ________ in initial prices.

5.18

Suppose that aggregate demand instead of increasing were to decrease. This would mean that at initial prices buyers would be willing to buy *(more/less)* output than before. Because the economy was initially at full employment, it also means that at initial prices buyers would be willing to purchase *(more/less)* output than could be produced.

Answers

14. potential · more
15. would not · would not
16. more · up
17. increase · aggregate demand · potential GNP
18. less · less

5.19

In this situation, if markets were to function perfectly, competition among producers would tend to drive prices *(up/down)* ________. In many markets, however, prices do not respond immediately to a decline in expenditure. Although industries generally respond to an increase in expenditure when there is full employment by raising ________________, many appear to be unwilling to cut prices when there is a decline in ________________.

5.20

If you look at Figures 5.1 and 5.2, you will see, for example, that during the period 1958–1965 actual GNP was *(less than/equal to)* ________ potential GNP, and the price level *(did/didnot)* ________ fall.

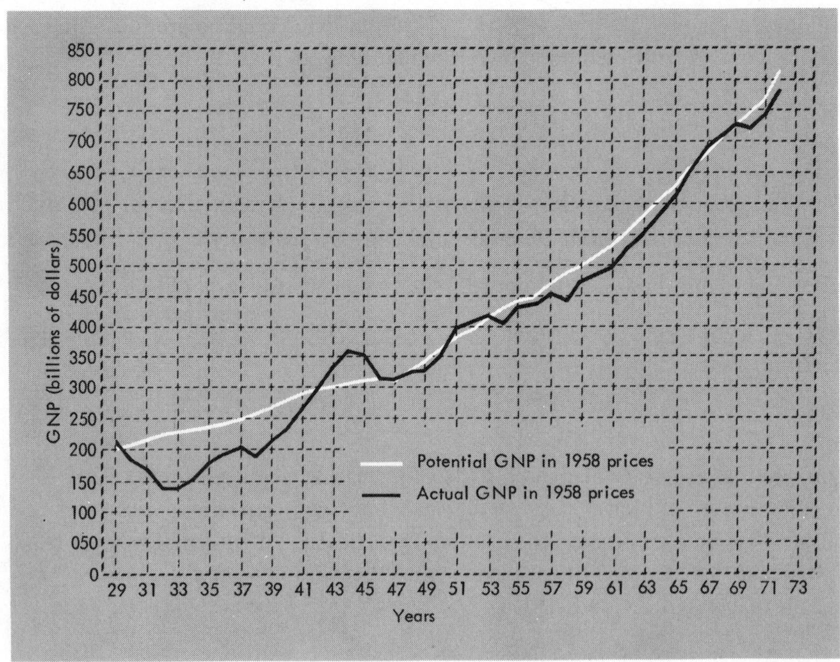

FIGURE 5.1 Real GNP and potential GNP, 1929–1972 (1958 prices)

Answers

19. down · prices · expenditure
20. less than · did not

5.21

Does this imply that no prices fell during this period? _(yes/no)_ ______ . It only implies that when aggregate demand was less than potential GNP in initial prices, the average ______________ ______________ did not fall.

5.22

In most other periods, when actual GNP fell below potential GNP the price level did not fall. As a result, it is possible to conclude that when aggregate demand falls below potential GNP in initial prices, the price level tends to be _(flexible/rigid)_ ______ .

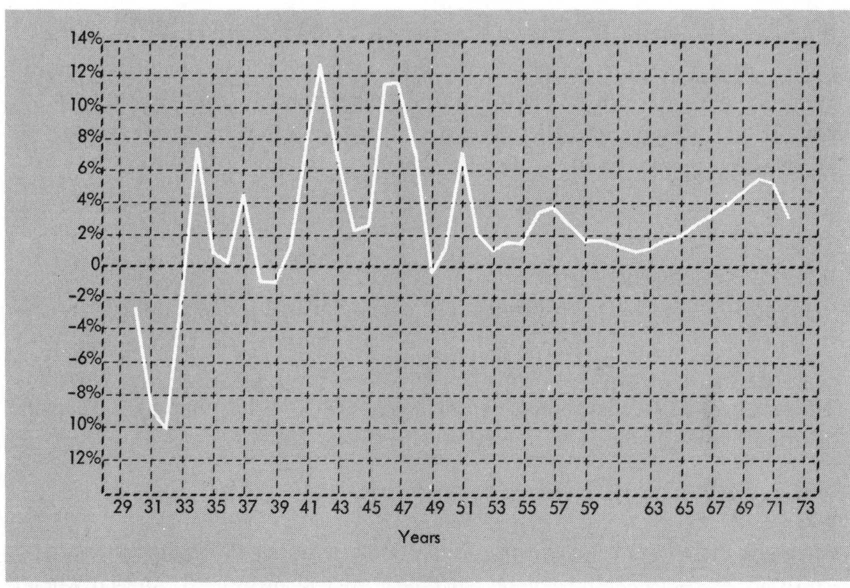

FIGURE 5.2 Change in GNP deflator, 1930–1972

5.23

A careful look at Figures 5.1 and 5.2 will reveal that for most years when actual GNP was less than potential GNP not only did the official price index not fall but it actually rose. It should be recalled, however, that because the GNP de-

Answers

21. no · price level
22. rigid

flator fails to fully take account of changes in the ______________ of output, it *(under/over)* ______ states the rate of inflation by about 1 or 2 percent. It is for this reason that a small rate of increase in the GNP deflator, as occurred in the 1958–1965 period, *(is/is not)* ______ considered by many to be true inflation.

5.24

The price level is not perfectly rigid when there is unemployment. It is possible for the price level to fall in such periods. If you look at Figure 5.1, you will see that in the 1930–1933 period actual GNP *(remained equal to/fell far below)* potential GNP. This was a period, then, in which aggregate demand fell very sharply and in which there was *(great/little)* ______ downward pressure on prices.

5.25

If you look at Figure 5.2, you will see that in 1930–1933 the price level *(rose/fell)* ______ quite sharply. From this evidence, it can be concluded that even though the price level tends not to fall when there is as much as 6 or 7 percent unemployment, if there is enough downward pressure on prices, the price level *(will/will not)* ______ decline.

5.26

It is also possible when there is unemployment for the price level to rise faster than the 1 or 2 percent considered to be consistent with price stability. Three such periods were 1934, 1937, and 1970–1972. In those years, there was *(high/low)* ______ unemployment, yet the price level *(rose/fell)* ______ sharply. The reasons for price level increases when actual GNP is less than potential will be discussed in Chapter 12.

5.27

Although there have been exceptions, particularly in the 1930s, and more recently in 1970–1972, the general pattern of price changes has been that when actual GNP falls below potential GNP the ______________ level stays relatively stable. In the model to be analyzed in this and following chapters, we will assume for the sake of simplicity that it is always true that when actual GNP is less than potential GNP, the price level *(will/will not)* ______ change.

Answers

23. quality · over · is not
24. fell far below · great
25. fell · will
26. high · rose
27. price · will not

5.28

Previously, it was concluded that when aggregate demand exceeds potential GNP in initial prices, the price level will *(rise/fall)*. In the model to be analyzed here, the same result will hold. Thus, in both the real world and in the model analyzed here, the price level will rise when ______ ______ exceeds ______ ______.

5.29

In the real world, the price level sometimes increases when aggregate demand is below potential GNP. In the model used here, however, it will be assumed that this will not occur. Thus, in the real world the price level has *(sometimes/never)* risen when aggregate demand is less than potential GNP in initial prices, but in the model it will be assumed that in this situation the price level *(will/will not)* rise.

5.30

In summary, the model discussed below assumes that whenever aggregate demand is greater than potential GNP, the price level is *(flexible/rigid)* and prices will *(rise/stay the same)*. It further assumes that the price level *(will/will not)* rise under other circumstances.

5.31

If the economy were initially at full employment, a decline in aggregate demand would mean that at initial prices buyers would want to buy *(more/less)* output than could be produced.

5.32

If prices were to remain at their initial level when aggregate demand falls, producers *(would/would not)* be able to sell as much output as before. As a result, it would no longer be profitable for them to use as large a quantity of resources and produce as much ______ as before.

Answers

28. rise · aggregate demand · potential GNP
29. sometimes · will not
30. flexible · rise · will not
31. less
32. would not · output

5.33

What this example shows is that when aggregate demand falls below potential GNP valued in initial prices, if there is downward price rigidity, some resources become ______________ and actual GNP falls below its ______________ .

5.34

Thus, according to our model, unemployment results when ______________ ______________ falls below ______________ ______________ in initial prices.

5.35

In summary, our model suggests that whether there will be inflation, unemployment, or full employment with no inflation depends on the level of ______________ ______________ relative to ______________ ______________ valued in initial prices.

a. If there is excess aggregate demand, the result will be ______________ .

b. If there is insufficient aggregate demand, the result will be ______________ .

c. If aggregate demand is just equal to potential output in initial prices, the result will be ______________ ______________ without ______________ .

5.36

Thus, the condition of the economy depends critically on the level of ______________ ______________ . The level of GNP that will result from different levels of aggregate demand can be summarized in terms of Figure 5.3.

5.37

In Figure 5.3, the horizontal axis measures ______________ ______________ in initial prices. Each point along the axis indicates an amount of real GNP equal to its distance from the origin.

Answers

33. unemployed · potential
34. aggregate demand · potential GNP
35. aggregate demand · potential GNP
    a. inflation
    b. unemployment
    c. full employment · inflation
36. aggregate demand
37. real GNP

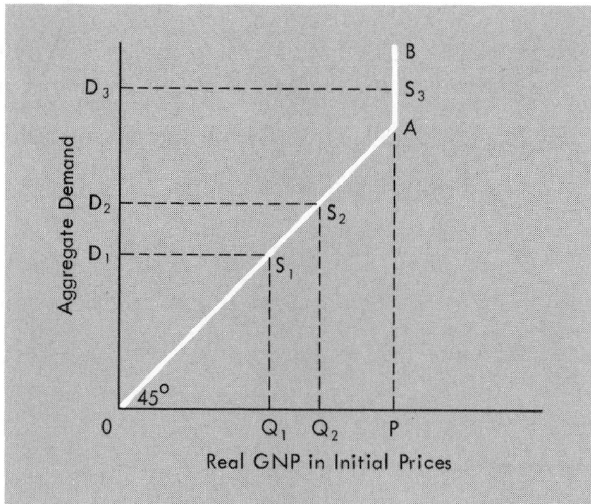

FIGURE 5.3 Aggregate supply

5.38

For example, the point Q_1 indicates an amount of real GNP equal to the distance from 0 to Q_1. This amount can be written simply $0Q_1$. Clearly, Q_2 indicates a *(larger/smaller)* GNP than Q_1 because $0Q_2$ is a *(greater/smaller)* distance than $0Q_1$.

5.39

Point P along the horizontal axis indicates the level of potential GNP. Thus, for the economy represented in Figure 5.3 the largest possible real GNP that can be attained is the distance ____________.

5.40

The vertical axis in Figure 5.3 measures ____________ ____________, which is the total ____________ that would be made at initial prices. Point D_3, for example, indicates a level of aggregate demand equal to ____________. The distance D_2D_3 shows how much greater $0D_3$ is than *(D_2D_3/$0D_2$)*.

Answers

38. larger · greater
39. 0P
40. aggregate demand · expenditure · $0D_3$ · $0D_2$

5.41

In Figure 5.3, there is a kinked line that starts at 0, goes to A, and then rises vertically to B. This line 0AB shows the level of real GNP in initial prices (which is shown along the ________ axis) that will result for each possible level of aggregate demand (which is shown along the ________ axis).

5.42

Line 0AB is called the *aggregate supply* curve. It shows the level of real GNP in initial prices that will be supplied for each possible level of ________ ________.

5.43

If you know the level of aggregate demand, you can find what the level of real GNP will be from the ________ ________ curve.

5.44

For example, in Figure 5.3, suppose the level of aggregate demand is $0D_1$. The point on the aggregate supply curve that corresponds to that level of aggregate demand is ________. This point lies directly above point ________ on the horizontal axis. This indicates that the level of real GNP that will be supplied is ________.

5.45

As is indicated in Figure 5.3, the segment 0A of the aggregate supply curve makes a ________ degree angle with each axis. Because of this, any level of aggregate demand that corresponds to a point on 0A will result in a real GNP of an equal amount. For example, $0D_1$ is the same amount as ________.

Answers

41. horizontal · vertical
42. aggregate demand
43. aggregate supply
44. S_1 · Q_1 · $0Q_1$
45. 45 · $0Q_1$

5.46

If aggregate demand were to increase from $0D_1$ to $0D_2$, real GNP would increase from ________ to ________. Because line 0A is a 45 degree line, the increase in aggregate demand, $D_1 D_2$, results in an equal increase in real GNP, ________.

5.47

As you will recall, in this model when aggregate demand falls below potential GNP in initial prices, the price level is *(flexible/inflexible)*. As a result, a decline in aggregate demand will cause an equal decline in *(output/prices)*. This is represented in Figure 5.3 by the 45 degree line, along which a change in aggregate demand is accompanied by an ________ change in real GNP.

5.48

A fall in aggregate demand below potential GNP in initial prices will reduce *(output/prices)* instead of *(output/prices)*. An increase in aggregate demand from a level below potential GNP in initial prices will increase output instead of prices.

5.49

That is, when there is unemployment, an increase in aggregate demand *(will/will not)* lead producers to increase prices. Instead, producers will hire more ________ and produce more ________ to match the increase in aggregate demand. Again, this is represented by the 45 degree line, along which an increase in aggregate demand is accompanied by an ________ increase in real GNP.

5.50

Thus, when there is unemployment, prices are *(rigid/flexible)*, and the aggregate supply curve is a *(45 degree/vertical)* line.

Answers

46. $0Q_1$ · $0Q_2$ · Q_1Q_2
47. inflexible · output · equal
48. output · prices
49. will not · resources · output · equal
50. rigid · 45 degree

5.51

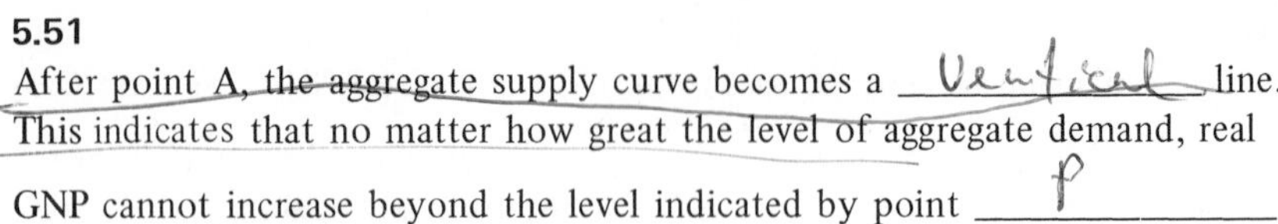

After point A, the aggregate supply curve becomes a ____________ line. This indicates that no matter how great the level of aggregate demand, real GNP cannot increase beyond the level indicated by point ____________, which is directly below point A.

5.52

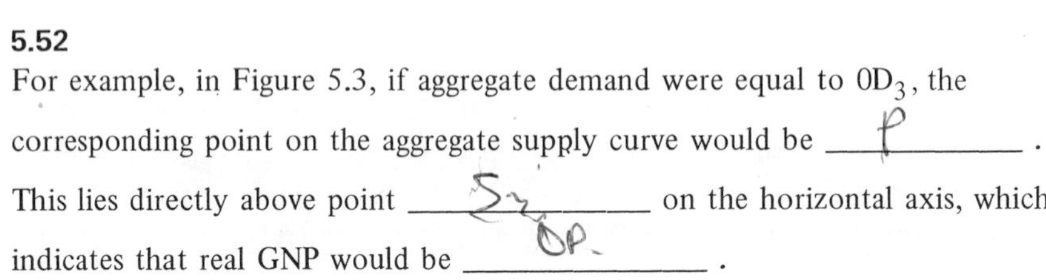

For example, in Figure 5.3, if aggregate demand were equal to $0D_3$, the corresponding point on the aggregate supply curve would be ____________. This lies directly above point ____________ on the horizontal axis, which indicates that real GNP would be ____________.

5.53

The reason that the aggregate supply curve becomes a vertical line above point P is that 0P is the level of potential GNP. No matter how great the level of aggregate demand, real GNP cannot exceed ____________ GNP. Even if aggregate demand were greater than $0D_3$, the level of real GNP indicated by the aggregate supply curve would still be ____________, which is equal to potential GNP.

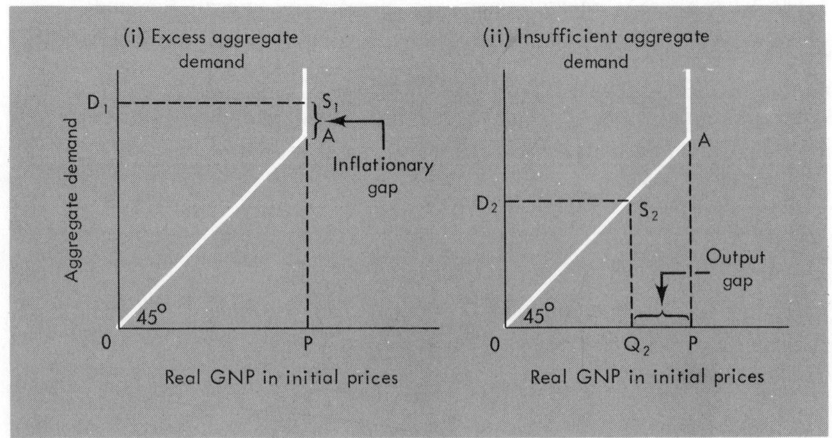

FIGURE 5.4 Aggregate supply

Answers

51. vertical · P
52. S_3 · P · 0P
53. potential · 0P

5.54

The difference between having too much and too little aggregate demand can be seen in Figure 5.4, which shows two typical cases. Here, as in Figure 5.3, the vertical axis measures ________ ________, and the horizontal axis measures ________ ________ in initial prices. Again, the aggregate supply curve has two segments: one makes a ________ degree angle with each axis at the origin, and the other is a vertical line above point P on the horizontal axis that indicates the level of ________ GNP.

5.55

In case (i), the level of aggregate demand is $0D_1$. This corresponds to point ________, which is also the level of ________ GNP. Because real GNP is 0P, in this case, there *(will/will not)* be full employment.

5.56

Because S_1 is on the vertical segment of the aggregate supply curve, you know that $0D_1$ is *(greater/smaller)* than 0P. This means that aggregate demand is *(greater/smaller)* than potential GNP.

5.57

The amount by which aggregate demand exceeds potential GNP is ________. Because excess aggregate demand leads to ________, this amount is called, as noted in Figure 5.4, the ________ gap.

5.58

Whenever there is an ________ gap, it means that the amount of output that consumers, businesses, and governments would be willing to buy at initial prices is *(greater/smaller)* than the output that can be produced with available resources. The result in such a situation will be *(unemployment/full employment)* with ________.

Answers

54. aggregate demand · real GNP · 45 · potential
55. S_1 · 0P · potential · will
56. greater · greater
57. AS_1 · inflation · inflationary
58. inflationary · greater · full employment · inflation

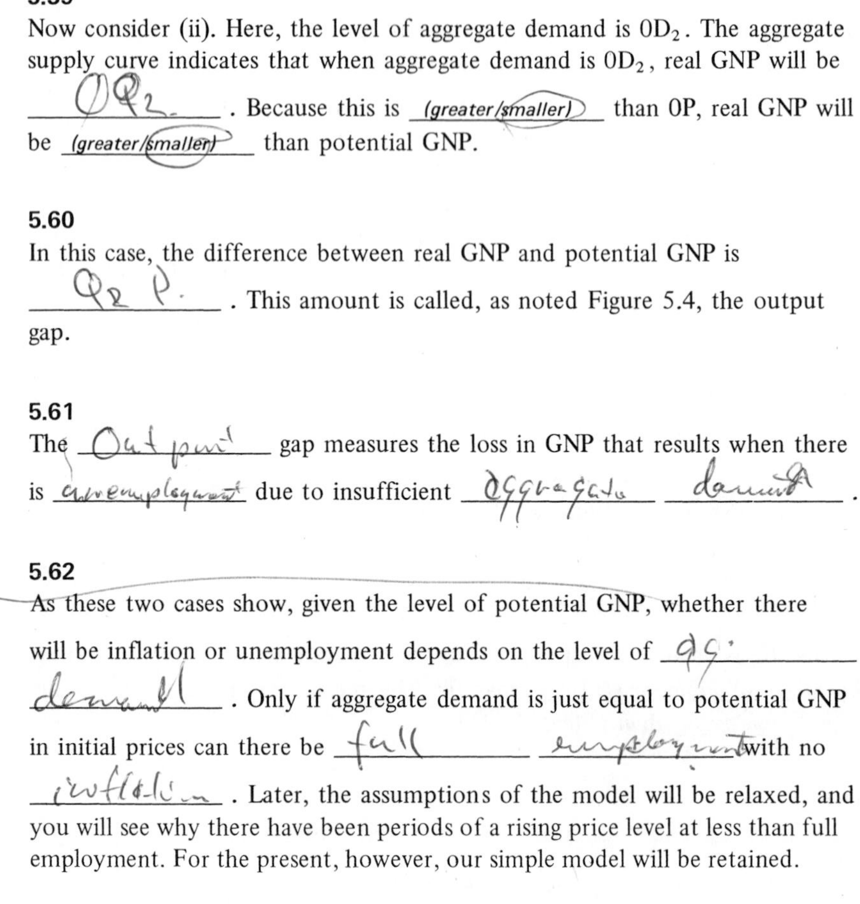

5.59

Now consider (ii). Here, the level of aggregate demand is $0D_2$. The aggregate supply curve indicates that when aggregate demand is $0D_2$, real GNP will be ______. Because this is *(greater/smaller)* than 0P, real GNP will be *(greater/smaller)* than potential GNP.

5.60

In this case, the difference between real GNP and potential GNP is ______. This amount is called, as noted Figure 5.4, the output gap.

5.61

The ______ gap measures the loss in GNP that results when there is ______ due to insufficient ______ ______.

5.62

As these two cases show, given the level of potential GNP, whether there will be inflation or unemployment depends on the level of ______ ______. Only if aggregate demand is just equal to potential GNP in initial prices can there be ______ ______ with no ______. Later, the assumptions of the model will be relaxed, and you will see why there have been periods of a rising price level at less than full employment. For the present, however, our simple model will be retained.

REVIEW QUESTIONS

5.1

Whether there will be unemployment or inflation is determined by:

a. the level of aggregate demand.
b. the level of potential GNP.

Answers

59. $0Q_2$ · smaller · smaller
60 Q_2P
61. output · unemployment · aggregate demand
62. aggregate demand · full employment · inflation

c. the size of the output gap relative to the inflationary gap.
d. the level of aggregate demand relative to potential GNP.

Aggregate demand is the expenditure that would be made at initial prices, and potential GNP is the output that could be produced if all resources were utilized. If aggregate demand exceeds potential GNP, the result will be inflation; if it falls short of potential GNP, the result will be unemployment. To know only the level of aggregate demand or only the level of potential GNP would not be sufficient to know whether inflation or unemployment would result. It is impossible for there to be both inflationary and output gaps at the same time because aggregate demand cannot both exceed and fall short of potential GNP at the same time. The correct response is d.

5.2
Which of the following explains why an increase in aggregate demand does not always lead to an equal increase in real GNP?

1. Potential GNP is an upper limit to real GNP.
2. There is not a sufficient quantity of resources to produce all levels of real GNP.
3. Resource owners and firms may respond by raising resource and product prices instead of producing more output.
   a. 1 and 2 only
   b. 1 and 3 only
   c. 2 and 3 only
   d. 1, 2, and 3

By definition, *potential GNP* is the amount of output that would be produced if all resources were utilized. This means that real GNP cannot exceed potential GNP because there are not enough resources to produce at a higher level. Thus, statements 1 and 2 must be correct explanations. Whenever aggregate demand exceeds potential GNP, there will be an excess demand in the market for at least some resources and products. Consequently, prices in these markets will rise, and statement 3 is a correct explanation. The correct response is d.

5.3
Which of the following explains why considerable unemployment can exist in a market economy?

a. At full employment, national income is not always sufficient to purchase all output produced.

b. Many product and factor prices respond very slowly when supply exceeds demand.
c. The rate of productivity increase is not always great enough to permit sufficient growth of actual output.
d. The growth of productive capacity outstrips the growth of consumers' private wants.

Other things equal, the lower the price of a good or resource, the larger the quantity demanded. Thus, if prices were completely flexible and responded quickly to situations of excess demand and excess supply, all markets including the labor market would clear. That is, full employment, apart from frictional elements, would always exist. Of the other options, none makes sense. By definition, national income equals national output. If the rate of productivity increase limited the growth of actual output, it would mean the economy was at full employment, and to date no nation has sufficient resources to satisfy all of its citizens' private wants. The correct response is b.

5.4

Which of the following features must a good economics model have in order to help us understand the economy?

1. It must be completely realistic.
2. It must be simple enough to understand.
3. It must capture some essential feature of the economy.
   a. 1 and 2 only
   b. 1 and 3 only
   c. 2 and 3 only
   d. 1, 2 and 3

The use of simple economic models to explain economic events in the real world is made necessary by the fact that the real world economy is very complex. There are so many interrelationships that it would be impossible to consider and understand them all at one time. Good models in economics are designed to explain only a limited number of phenomena at one time. Consequently, a good model need capture only that part of reality pertinent to the issue under consideration. It is not necessary, for example, for a model that is designed to explain the causes of inflation and unemployment to also explain the distribution of income and the allocation of resources. The correct response is c.

6

Equilibrium GNP

6.1
In the preceding chapter, it was concluded that whether there is inflation or unemployment depends on the relationship between ________________ ________________ and ________________ ________________ in initial prices.

6.2
If aggregate demand exceeds potential GNP in initials prices, there will be ________________ . If aggregate demand falls short of potential GNP in initial prices, there will be ________________ . Only if there is neither excess nor insufficient ________________ ________________ can there be full employment without inflation.

Answers

1. aggregate demand · potential GNP
2. inflation · unemployment · aggregate demand

6.3
What determines the level of aggregate demand? You will recall that aggregate demand is the total ______________ that consumers, businesses, and governments would make if prices were to remain unchanged. In other words, it is the sum of consumption, investment, and government expenditures at initial prices.

6.4
Consider consumption expenditure first. Clearly, many factors influence how much any family will spend on goods and services: family size, the ages of its members, preferences, and so on. But one factor that explains most of the differences in expenditure among different families is *income*. The more income a family has, the ___*(more/less)*___ it is likely to spend.

6.5
When considering the total expenditure of all consumers, the same factor explains most of the changes that have occurred over time. The principal reason that consumption expenditure has increased over time is that consumers' total ______________ has increased.

6.6
As we have seen, the total income that consumers have available to spend is called *disposable income*. The greater ______________ income is, the greater total ______________ expenditure is likely to be.

6.7
Although the level of consumption expenditure in any year depends on the level of ______________ income, it is not necessarily and not usually equal to it. Because on the average people save part of their income, consumption expenditure is usually ___*(more/less)*___ than disposable income.

Answers

3. expenditure
4. more
5. income
6. disposable · consumption
7. disposable · less

6.8

Because consumption expenditure depends on disposable income, it can be said that consumption expenditure is a *function* of disposable income. For this reason, the relationship between consumption expenditure and disposable income is called the *consumption function.* The consumption _______________ indicates, for any level of disposable income, what the level of ____________ _______________ will be. The consumption function can be shown diagrammatically, as in Figure 6.1. In this diagram, the horizontal axis measures _______________ _______________, and the vertical axis measures _______ _______________.

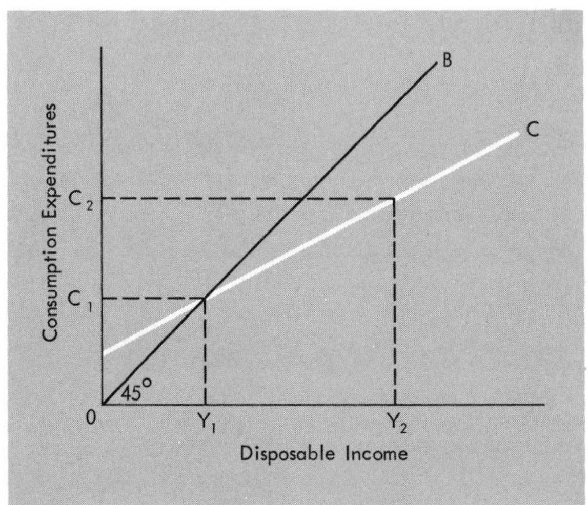

FIGURE 6.1 The consumption function

6.9

Because the line 0B is a 45 degree line from the origin, any point along that line shows amounts of consumption expenditure and disposable income that are _______________.

Answers

8. function · consumption expenditure · disposable income · consumption expenditure
9. equal

6.10

Line C is the consumption function. It shows for any level of disposable income what the level of _______________ _______________ will be. For example, if disposable income is $0Y_2$, consumption expenditure will be _______________.

6.11

For each level of disposable income, line 0B shows the consumption expenditure that would result if all income were spent. If disposable income is $0Y_2$, consumption expenditure is *(more/less)* than income, and part of income $0Y_2$ will be saved. The amount saved out of $0Y_2$ will be the vertical distance between line 0B and the _______________ function.

6.12

If disposable income is $0Y_1$, *(all/not all)* income will be spent because at this income level the consumption function and the 45 degree line intersect. For any level of disposable income less than $0Y_1$, consumption expenditure will be *(less/more)* than disposable income, and some consumers will spend part of their previous savings in addition to their disposable income.

6.13

As is shown by the _______________ _______________ in Figure 6.1, consumption expenditure depends on _______________ _______________.

6.14

Disposable income is closely related to the total income earned in the economy. As you will recall, in Chapter 3 it was emphasized that total income and the market value of total output must be _______________ because of the circular flow of income and expenditure. Therefore, disposable income must be related to the market value of total output, which is _______________.

Answers

10. consumption expenditure · $0C_2$
11. less · consumption
12. all · more
13. consumption function · disposable income
14. equal · GNP

6.15

Disposable income is the income that ______________ have available to spend for goods and services. Therefore, if you subtract from GNP (or total income) the income retained by businesses and governments, you will be left with the income retained by consumers, which is ______________ ______________ .

6.16

The relationship between GNP and disposable income can be summarized as follows:

GNP		depreciation
less: income retained by businesses	=	+ profit − direct business taxes − dividends
less: income retained by governments	=	taxes − transfer payments
equals: __________ __________	=	wages, salaries, interest, rent + dividends − personal taxes + transfer payments

6.17

From the above tabulation, you can see that the income earned by each of the three groups in the economy *(is/is not)* the same as the income retained by each group.

6.18

The business sector, for example, keeps only part of the depreciation and profit that it earns on its investment in capital goods and land. Part is paid out to the government in the form of direct business ______________ , and part is paid out to the owners, who are also consumers, in the form of ______________ .

Answers

15. consumers · disposable income
16. disposable income
17. is not
18. taxes · dividends

6.19

The government sector, although it earns no income, obtains income that it can use for purchases of goods and services by collecting ________________ . In addition to indirect business taxes, it collects corporate taxes and personal taxes. The personal taxes include income and social security taxes.

6.20

Not all the income that the government receives in taxes is available to purchase goods and services because part is paid out to consumers in the form of ________________ ________________ . Thus, the income retained by governments is equal to ________________ minus ________________ ________________ .

6.21

Disposable income, which is the remaining part of GNP, is equal to the income earned by consumers plus the income transfers *from* businesses and governments minus the income transfer *to* the government. The income earned takes the form of wages and salaries, interest, and rents. The income transfers from businesses are ________________ , and the income transfers from governments are ________________ ________________ .

6.22

Put simply, disposable income equals ________________ minus the retained income of business, minus taxes, plus transfer payments. Everything else being the same, the greater GNP is, the *(greater/smaller)* disposable income will be.

6.23

Because the level of disposable income is closely related to the level of GNP, the consumption function can be constructed in terms of GNP as well as in terms of disposable income. Previously, the consumption function showed the consumption expenditure that would result for any level of ________________ ________________ . Taking into account the relationship between disposable

Answers

19. taxes
20. transfer payments · taxes · transfer payments
21. dividends · transfer payments
22. GNP · greater
23. disposable income

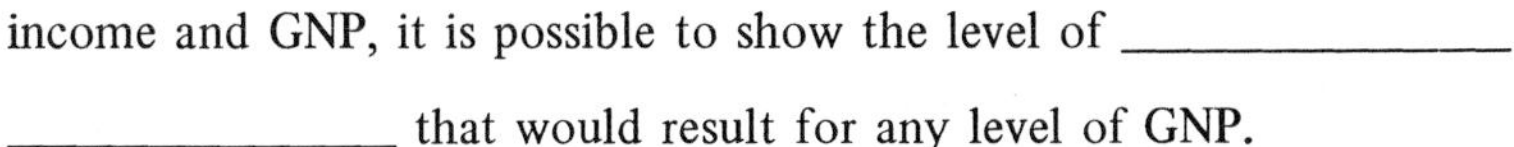

income and GNP, it is possible to show the level of ______________ ______________ that would result for any level of GNP.

6.24

The consumption function in terms of GNP is shown in Figure 6.2. This time the horizontal axis measures both ______________ ______________ and disposable income. The consumption function in terms of real GNP is shown by line C. If GNP were $0Q_1$, the consumption function indicates that consumption expenditure would be ______________ .

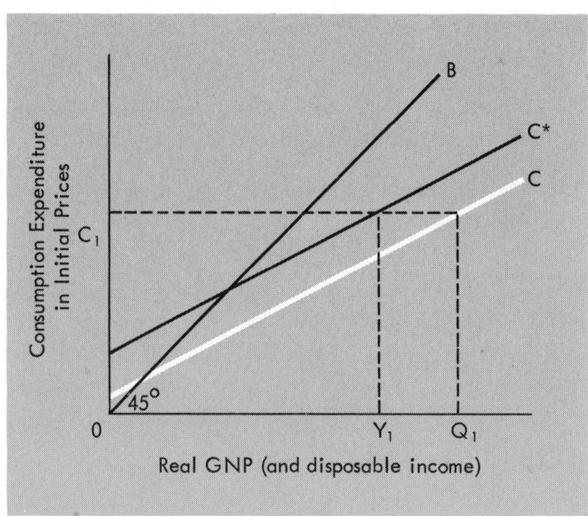

FIGURE 6.2 The consumption function

6.25

The line C* shows consumption expenditure when the horizontal axis is used to measure disposable income instead of GNP. Because disposable income is *(larger/smaller)* than GNP, any given amount of GNP, such as $0Q_1$, will be accompanied by a smaller amount of disposable income, such as $0Y_1$. The consumption expenditure indicated by C for a GNP of $0Q_1$ is ______________ . The consumption expenditure indicated by C* for disposable income $0Y_1$ ______________ be the same amount.

Answers

23. consumption expenditure
24. real GNP · $0C_1$
25. smaller · $0C_1$ · must

6.26

For this reason, C lies parallel to and to the *(left/right)* of C*. Suppose a disposable income of $500 billion results in consumption expenditure of $400 billion. Because GNP will be greater than disposable income, it will take a GNP that is *(more/less)* than $500 billion to generate $400 billion in consumption expenditure.

6.27

The consumption function C shows how one component of aggregate demand depends on the level of GNP. The higher real GNP, the *(higher/lower)* the expenditure that consumers would be willing to make at initial prices.

6.28

Suppose, for the sake of simplicity, that both investment expenditure and government expenditure were independent of the level of GNP. This means that whatever the level of GNP, ______________ and ______________ expenditures would be the same.

6.29

The independence of GNP for these two types of expenditures is shown in Figure 6.3. Diagram (i) shows the investment function I as a *(horizontal/vertical)* line. This indicates, for example, that whether GNP is $0Q_1$ or $0Q_2$ investment expenditure will be ______________ .

6.30

Diagram (ii) shows the government expenditure function G as a ______________ line. In this case, whether GNP is $0Q_1$, $0Q_2$, or any other amount, government expenditure will be ______________ .

Answers

26. right · more
27. higher
28. investment · government
29. horizontal · $0I_1$
30. horizontal · $0G_1$

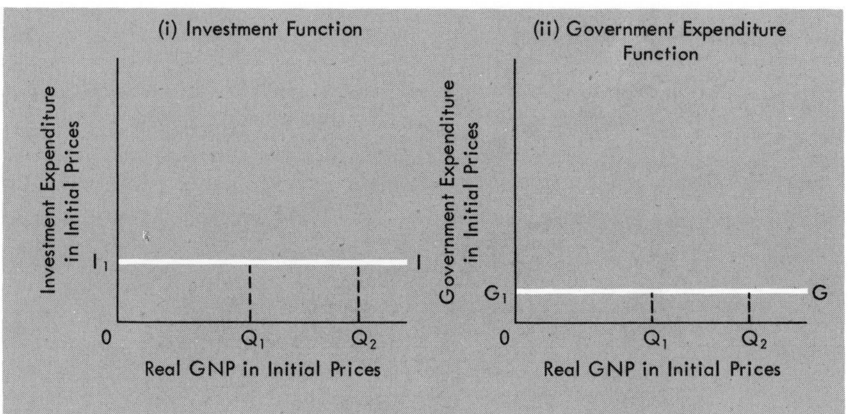

FIGURE 6.3 Investment and government expenditure

6.31

Because aggregate demand is the total ________________ that would be made at initial prices, it will be equal to the sum of ________________ , __________ and ________________ expenditures.

6.32

By adding together the consumption, investment, and government expenditures functions from Figures 6.2 and 6.3, it is possible to obtain an ________________ ________________ curve. This is shown as the AD curve in Figure 6.4.

6.33

In Figure 6.4, the C curve is, of course, the ________________ ________________ from Figure 6.2. It shows for different levels of real GNP the consumption ________________ that would be made by households.

Answers

31. expenditure · consumption · investment · government
32. aggregate demand
33. consumption function · expenditure

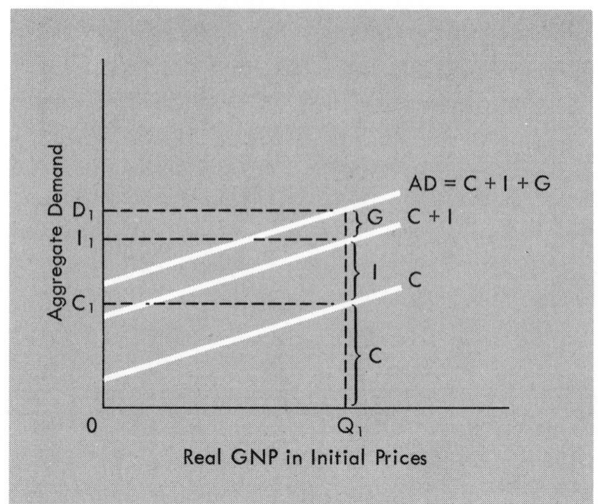

FIGURE 6.4 Aggregate demand

6.34

The C + I curve is obtained by adding to the consumption expenditure, given by the C curve for each level of real GNP, the _______________ expenditure given by the investment function shown in Figure 6.3 (i). The C + I curve shows the sum of consumption and investment expenditures that would be made by households and businesses for each level of _______________ _______________ in initial prices.

6.35

Finally, the AD curve is obtained by adding to the *(C/C + I)* curve the government expenditure given by the G curve in Figure 6.3 (ii). The AD curve shows the level of _______________ _______________ in initial prices.

6.36

Suppose real GNP were $0Q_1$. At this level of real GNP, consumption expenditure would be _______________, investment expenditure would be _______________, and government expenditures would be _______________.

Answers

34. investment · real GNP
35. C + I · aggregate demand · real GNP
36. $0C_1$ · C_1I_1 · I_1D_1

Aggregate demand, which would be the sum of these three, would be

______________ .

6.37

By putting the aggregate demand curve together with the aggregate supply curve from Figure 5.3, it is possible to see what level of real GNP will result, and whether there will be ______________ or ______________ . This is done in Figure 6.5.

6.38

In Figure 6.5, suppose that initially GNP were $0Q_0$–what would happen? At that level of real GNP, aggregate demand would be ______________ , which would be *(greater/less)*______ than real GNP. This means that the amount of output that buyers would want to buy at that level of real GNP is *(greater/less)*______ than the amount produced.

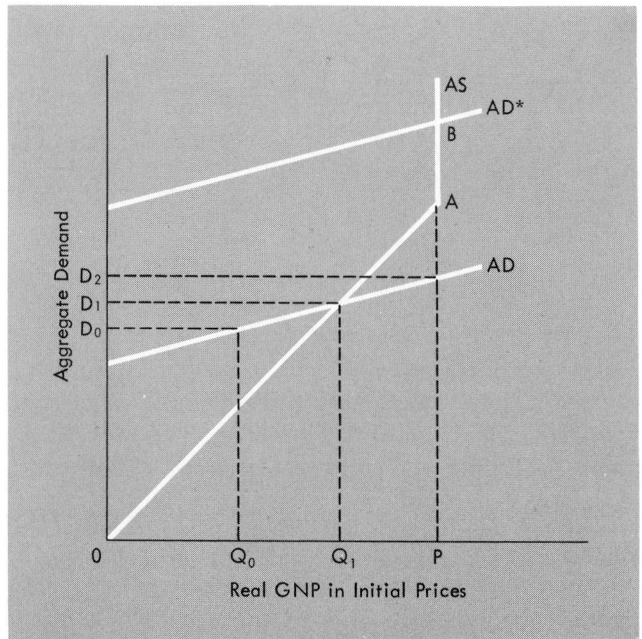

FIGURE 6.5 Aggregate demand and aggregate supply

Answers

36. $0D_1$
37. inflation · unemployment (either order)
38. $0D_0$ · greater · greater

6.39

At a real GNP of $0Q_0$, there will be ______________ resources. Because aggregate demand exceeds real GNP, producers *(will/will not)* hire more resources and will increase *(prices/output)* .

6.40

Thus, real GNP would not be maintained at $0Q_0$ because at that level aggregate demand would be *(greater/less)* than aggregate supply. The behavior of producers in such a situation would cause *(an increase/a decrease)* in real GNP.

6.41

As long as real GNP is less than $0Q_1$, aggregate demand will be *(greater/less)* than aggregate supply, and real GNP will *(increase/decrease)* .

6.42

Suppose real GNP were initially equal to 0P. Here, aggregate demand would be equal to ______________, which is *(greater/less)* than real GNP. Producers would find that they are producing more output than they can sell and will act to *(increase/decrease)* real GNP by reducing their employment of resources and producing less output.

6.43

As long as real GNP is greater than $0Q_1$, producers will act to *(increase/decrease)* GNP.

6.44

Because real GNP will increase if it is below $0Q_1$ and decrease if it is above $0Q_1$, it can be expected that real GNP will adjust to the level ______________.

Answers

39. unemployed · will · output
40. greater · an increase
41. greater · increase
42. $0D_2$ · less · decrease
43. decrease
44. $0Q_1$

This is the level where aggregate demand and aggregate supply are ______________ . This is the *equilibrium* level of real GNP.

6.45

The level of real GNP where aggregate demand and aggregate supply are equal is called the ______________ level of GNP. The economy is in equilibrium when there is no tendency to change. In Figure 6.5, it is clear that $0Q_1$ is the only ______________ level of real GNP.

6.46

Suppose, in Figure 6.5, that the AD curve were AD* and intersected the aggregate supply curve in the vertical segment AB. If this occurred, firms would find that at initial prices buyers would be willing to purchase *(more/less)* output than they could produce. Because firms could not expand production enough to match aggregate demand, the result would be *(unemployment/inflation)* .

6.47

In short, whether there is inflation, unemployment, or neither depends on the relative positions of the aggregate ______________ and ______________ curves.

6.48

Looking back to Figure 6.5, if the aggregate demand curve is AD*, there will be an ______________ gap of ______________ , whereas if the aggregate demand curve is AD, there will be an ______________ gap of ______________ .

6.49

In terms of the simple model of the economy shown in Figure 6.6, the equilibrium level of real GNP depends on where the aggregate demand curve intersects the aggregate supply curve.

Answers

44. equal
45. equilibrium · equilibrium
46. more · inflation
47. demand · supply (either order)
48. inflationary · AB · output · Q_1P

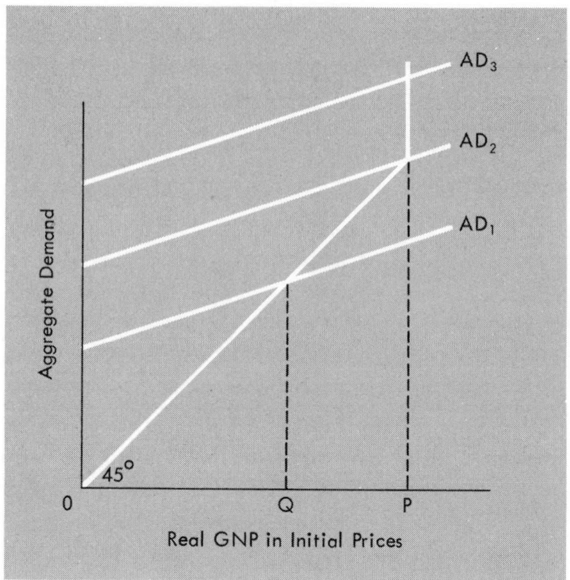

FIGURE 6.6 Aggregate demand and aggregate supply

For example, for aggregate demand curve AD_1, the equilibrium real GNP is

________________ .

6.50

If real GNP deviates from its equilibrium level, the amount of output that consumers, businesses, and governments would be willing to buy and the amount of output produced *(would/would not)* be equal. In such an event, producers would adjust production to match aggregate demand and real GNP would adjust to its ________________ level.

6.51

Thus, in Figure 6.6 real GNP cannot permanently diverge from 0Q as long as the aggregate demand curve is ________________ . Thus, ignoring temporary deviations from equilibrium, in order for real GNP to change it is necessary for the ________________ ________________ curve to shift.

Answers

49. 0Q
50. would not · equilibrium
51. AD_1 · aggregate demand

6.52

If the aggregate demand curve were to shift up from AD_1 to AD_2, real GNP would increase from ______________ to ______________ .

6.53

Similarly, if aggregate demand were initially AD_3, it would not be necessary to shift the aggregate demand curve to AD_1 in order to eliminate the excess aggregate demand. To do so would succeed in eliminating the excess aggregate demand, but would also cause ______________ .

6.54

In summary, the equilibrium level of real GNP depends on where the aggregate demand curve intersects the aggregate supply curve. In terms of the simple model shown in Figure 6.6, given the aggregate demand curve AD_1, the equilibrium real GNP is ______________ .

6.55

If real GNP deviates from its equilibrium level, the amount of output that consumers, businesses, and governments would be willing to buy and the amount of output produced *(would/would not)* be equal. In such an event, producers would adjust production to match aggregate demand, and real GNP would adjust to its ______________ level.

6.56

Thus, in Figure 6.6, real GNP cannot permanently diverge from 0Q as long as the aggregate demand curve is ______________ . Ignoring temporary deviations from equilibrium, in order for real GNP to change it is necessary for the ______________ ______________ curve to shift.

Answers

52. 0Q · 0P
53. unemployment
54. 0Q
55. would not · equilibrium
56. AD_1 · aggregate demand

REVIEW QUESTIONS

6.1

For a given level of GNP, the consumption expenditures that households would like to make depends on which of the following variables?

1. Taxes
2. Transfer payments.
3. Dividends.
   a. 1 and 2 only
   b. 3 only
   c. 1, 2, and 3
   d. neither 1, 2, nor 3

The consumption expenditure households in the aggregate would like to make depends on the level of disposable income. In Chapter 6, disposable income was shown to be equal to GNP minus the income retained by business and government. For a given level of GNP, the income retained by business decreases as dividends increase, and the income retained by government decreases as taxes decrease and transfer payments increase. Consequently, lower taxes, higher transfer payments and higher dividends will imply higher disposable income and consumption expenditure. The correct response is c.

6.2

If real GNP in initial prices increases, then aggregate demand will

a. decrease.
b. increase by a greater amount.
c. increase by the same amount.
d. increase by a smaller amount.

Aggregate demand is the expenditure that households, businesses, and government, taken together, would like to make at initial prices. In the simple model for the economy that has been used in this book, investment expenditure and government expenditure have been assumed to be independent of the level of real GNP. Consumption expenditure, however, is assumed to increase whenever real GNP increases, but only by a fraction of the increase in real GNP. Consequently, aggregate demand will increase in response to an increase in real GNP, but by a smaller amount. The correct response is d.

6.3

If real GNP is less than potential GNP, and aggregate demand and real GNP are not equal, then

a. aggregate demand will change, but actual GNP will stay the same.
b. actual GNP will change, but aggregate demand will stay the same.
c. both aggregate demand and actual GNP will change.
d. the economy is in equilibrium.

Because aggregate demand and real GNP are not equal and the economy is at less than full employment, the existing level of GNP is not an equilibrium level. Consequently, real GNP will tend to change. If aggregate demand is greater than real GNP, then real GNP will increase. This will cause aggregate demand to increase, although by a lesser amount. Both will continue to increase until they become equal or until actual GNP reaches potential GNP. If aggregate demand is less than real GNP, both will fall (aggregate demand less rapidly) until they become equal. The correct response is c.

6.4

Suppose actual GNP and potential GNP are equal, but aggregate demand and real GNP are not equal. In this situation, which of the following could result?

1. The average price level would tend to rise.
2. Total output would tend to fall.
   a. 1 only
   b. 2 only
   c. either 1 or 2
   d. neither 1 nor 2

Given that actual and potential output are equal, in order for the price level and total output to remain unchanged it is necessary for aggregate demand to be equal to real GNP. Because that condition is not satisfied, one or the other must change. Not enough information, however, is provided to determine which will change. If aggregate demand were greater than real GNP at full employment, then the price level would tend to rise. If aggregate demand were less than real GNP, total output would tend to fall. The correct response is c.

7

The Multiplier

7.1
In Chapters 5 and 6, you learned that, given potential GNP, the level of real GNP depends on the level of ________________ ________________ . If aggregate demand falls short of potential GNP in initial prices, then there will be ________________ . If aggregate demand exceeds potential GNP in initial prices, then there will be ________________ .

7.2
Aggregate demand is the total expenditure in initial prices made by consumers, businesses, and governments. The higher the level of real GNP in initial prices, the *(higher/lower)* the level of aggregate demand. One reason for this is that when there is an increase in real GNP, there is also an increase in ________________ income and, as a result, an increase in ________________ expenditure.

Answers

1. aggregate demand · unemployment · inflation
2. higher · disposable · consumption

7.3

An increase in real GNP will result in an increase in _______________ _______________. Such a change in aggregate demand is called an *induced* change in expenditure because it is induced, or caused, by the change in _______________ _______________.

7.4

An increase in aggregate demand that is caused by factors other than an increase in real GNP is called an *autonomous* change in expenditure. The difference between an induced and an autonomous change in aggregate demand is that an _______________ change is caused by a change in real GNP, whereas an _______________ change is caused by some other factor.

7.5

If consumption expenditure and, therefore, aggregate demand increase because of an increase in real GNP, this would be an _______________ increase in aggregate demand. If investment expenditure increases because a survey of consumers' spending intentions makes businesses more optimistic about future demand for their output, this would be an _______________ increase in aggregate demand.

7.6

In terms of the aggregate demand curve, a movement along the curve as real GNP changes is an _______________ change in aggregate demand.

7.7

How would an autonomous change in aggregate demand be represented diagramatically? Suppose that all of a sudden consumers decided to consume more of their income. This means that at any level of real GNP, total consumption expenditure would be *(higher/lower)* than it was before. Or, in other words, the consumption function would shift *(upward/downward)*.

Answers

3. aggregate demand · real GNP
4. induced · autonomous
5. induced · autonomous
6. induced
7. higher · upward

7.8
Such a change in consumers' behavior is represented in Figure 7.1 (i), in which the ______________ ______________ shifts from C_1 to C_2. Because aggregate demand is the sum of consumption, investment, and government expenditures, a shift in the consumption function from C_1 to C_2 will cause the ______________ ______________ curve to ______________ from AD_1 to AD_2. This assumes, of course, *(an/no)* autonomous change in investment and government expenditures.

7.9
In this example, a change in aggregate demand due to a change in consumers' preferences resulted in a *(shift in/movement along)* the aggregate demand curve. In fact, any ______________ change in consumption expenditure will result in a shift in the aggregate demand curve.

7.10
Suppose consumers became worried about a possible depression, and they decided to save more and consume less of their present income in order to provide for that "rainy day." This would be an ______________ change in expenditure and would result in a *(shift in/movement along)* both the consumption function and the aggregate demand curve.

7.11
Suppose that the depression did come, and the decline in GNP and disposable income caused consumption expenditure to decline. This would be an ______________ change in expenditure and would result in a *(shift in/movement along)* both the consumption function and the aggregate demand curve.

7.12
Changes in investment expenditure can be analyzed in the same way. You will recall that for the sake of simplicity we assumed investment expenditure was *(dependent on/independent of)* the level of real GNP. In terms of induced and

Answers

8. consumption function · aggregate demand · shift · no
9. shift in · autonomous
10. autonomous · shift in
11. induced · movement along
12. independent of

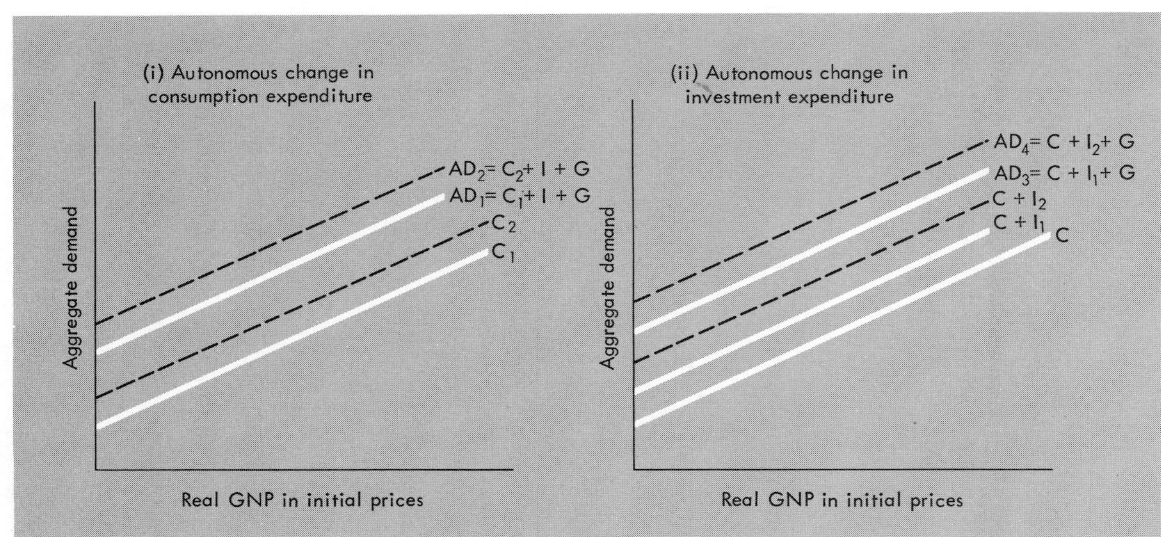

FIGURE 7.1 Autonomous changes in aggregate demand

autonomous changes in expenditure, we assumed that there were no _______________ changes in expenditure. Consequently, in our simplified analysis we will consider only _______________ changes in investment expenditure.

7.13

Suppose that a series of new inventions makes investment in capital goods more profitable to undertake. This increase in the profitability on investment means that, for any level of GNP, businesses will want to make *(greater/less)* investment expenditure than before. As a result, the investment _______________ will shift up.

7.14

In terms of Figure 7.1 (ii), even though the _______________ function remains unchanged, the shift in the _______________ function raises the $C + I_1$ curve to $C + I_2$ and the aggregate demand curve from _______________ to _______________ .

7.15

What is the effect of an autonomous change in aggregate demand? In Figure 7.2, an autonomous increase is represented by an upward shift in the aggregate demand curve from AD_1 to AD_2. The amount of this shift, as is shown on the vertical axis, is _______________ .

7.16

The effect of this upward shift in the aggregate demand curve will be to shift its point of intersection with the aggregate supply curve from _______________ to _______________ . This indicates that, as a result of the shift from AD_1 to AD_2, equilibrium aggregate demand will increase from _______________ to _______________ .

Answers

12. induced · autonomous
13. greater · function
14. consumption · investment · AD_3 · AD_4
15. D_1D_2
16. A · H · OD_1 · OD_3

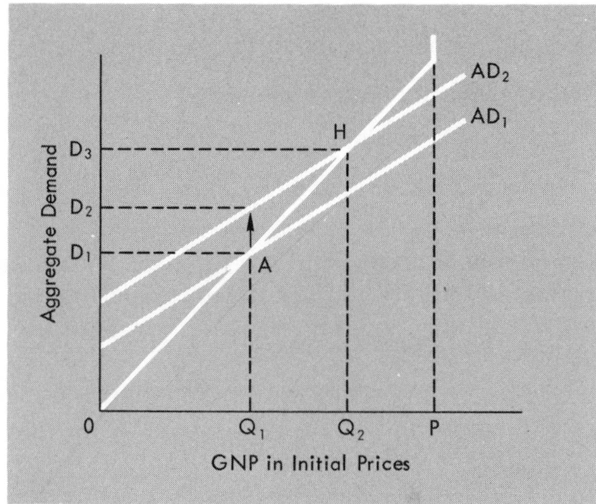

FIGURE 7.2 Autonomous and induced changes in aggregate demand

7.17

Thus, the autonomous increase in aggregate demand of ______________ will lead to a total increase in aggregate demand of ______________ . As you can clearly see, the total increase is *(greater than/equal to)* the autonomous increase. And, because there is unemployment, the increase in real GNP will be *(greater than/equal to)* the autonomous increase in aggregate demand.

7.18

How is it that an autonomous increase in aggregate demand can lead to a greater total increase in aggregate demand and real GNP? Because there is unemployment, the autonomous increase in aggregate demand will lead, at first, to an equal increase in ______________ ______________ . But that increase in real GNP will induce a further increase in aggregate demand. That is, an autonomous increase in aggregate demand will lead to an increase in real GNP that, in turn, will lead to an ______________ increase in aggregate demand.

Answers

17. D_1D_2 · D_1D_3 · greater than · greater than
18. real GNP · induced

7.19

Now, the induced increase in aggregate demand will lead to a further increase in real GNP, which will in turn lead to another ______________ increase in aggregate demand.

7.20

This process can be seen in Figure 7.3. Here, the autonomous increase in aggregate demand of AB will lead, at first, to an equal increase in real GNP of ______________ . This in turn will lead to an induced increase in aggregate demand of ______________ , which will lead to a further increase in real GNP of ______________ . This will continue until point ______________ is reached.

7.21

The total increase in aggregate demand will be AB, which is the ______________ increase, plus CD, EF, and so on, which are the ______________ changes in aggregate demand.

7.22

Similarly, the increase in real GNP will be the sum of ______________ , ______________ , ______________ , and so on.

7.23

As Figure 7.3 makes clear, an autonomous change in aggregate demand will have a multiplied effect on real GNP. This multiplied effect is called the *multiplier.* The multiplier shows how many times greater the total increase in real GNP will be than an ______________ increase in aggregate demand.

Answers

19. induced
20. BC · CD · DE · H
21. autonomous · induced
22. BC · DE · FG
23. autonomous

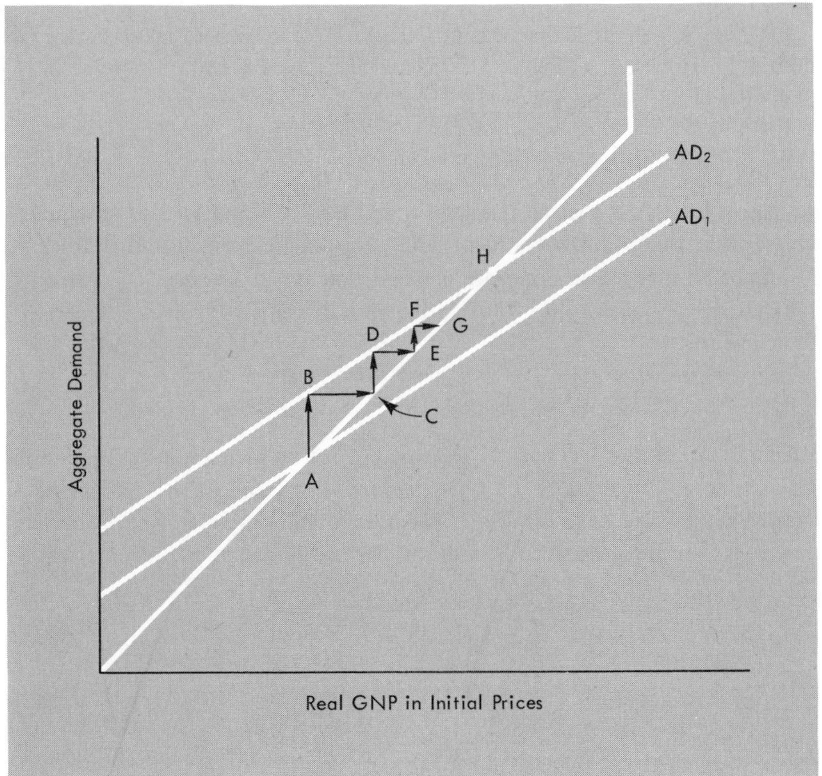

FIGURE 7.3 The multiplier

7.24

If an autonomous increase in aggregate demand of $10 billion will cause a total increase in real GNP of $30 billion, the _______________ is 3. If an autonomous decrease in aggregate demand of $5 billion will cause a total decrease in real GNP of $10 billion, the _______________ is _______________.

7.25

The reason there is a multiplier is that an autonomous increase in aggregate demand leads to an increase in real GNP, which leads to an _______________ increase in aggregate demand, which leads to an increase in _______________ _______________, which leads to . . . and so on.

Answers

24. multiplier · multiplier · 2
25. induced · real GNP

7.26

At first, you might think that this process would continue to increase real GNP indefinitely. However, as Figure 7.3 makes clear, each round of increase in real GNP will be ___*(larger/smaller)*___ than the preceding one.

7.27

The reason for this is that an increase in real GNP will not lead to an equal increase in consumption, investment, and government expenditures. Rather, it will induce an increase in aggregate demand that is ___*(greater/less)*___ than itself. That is, ___*(all/not all)*___ of an increase in real GNP (or total income) will be spent.

7.28

In general, consumers will spend ___*(part/all)*___ of an increase in disposable income and save ___*(part/none)*___. The increase in consumption expenditure divided by the increase in disposable income is called the *marginal propensity to consume,* or *MPC.* Because part of an increase in disposable income will be saved, the ______________ must be less than 1.

7.29

For simplicity, it will be assumed here that all of any increase in real GNP will take the form of an increase in disposable income. Under this assumption, the induced increase in consumption expenditure divided by the increase in real GNP will be the ______________. For example, if an increase in real GNP of $3 billion will induce an increase in consumption expenditure of $2 billion, the MPC is ______________. In general,

$$\frac{\text{the change in consumption expenditure}}{\text{the change in real GNP}} = \underline{\hspace{4cm}},$$

or, using the symbol Δ for "change in,"

$$\frac{\Delta C}{\Delta GNP} = \underline{\hspace{4cm}}.$$

Answers

26. smaller
27. less · not all
28. part · part · MPC
29. MPC · 2/3 · MPC · MPC

7.30

The MPC tells you how much _(autonomous/induced)_ consumption expenditure will result from a change in real GNP. If the MPC is 1/2, a decrease in real GNP of $100 billion will cause a decrease in consumption expenditure of

$ ______________ billion.

7.31

Under the simplified assumption that investment expenditure was independent of real GNP, an increase in real GNP would not result in any ______________ investment expenditure. Similarly, government expenditure is not considered to change systematically with changes in real GNP. Following this assumption, an increase in real GNP _(will/will not)_ induce an increase in government expenditure.

7.32

Thus, the amount of induced aggregate demand that results from an increase in real GNP depends on the ______________ . For example, if the MPC is 0.7, an increase in real GNP of $10 billion will induce an increase in consumption expenditure of $ ______________ billion and in aggregate demand

$ ______________ billion.

7.33

Because the induced change in consumption is less than the change in the real GNP that caused it, the MPC is _(less than/equal to/greater than)_ 1. It is because MPC is less than ______________ that, in the multiplier process, the successive increases in real GNP become _(larger/smaller)_ . This can be seen in Table 7.1, which shows the multiplier effect of an ______________ increase in investment expenditure of 10 when the MPC is 0.5. In this example, it will be assumed that there is a sufficient quantity of unemployed resources so that an increase in aggregate demand will result in an equal increase in ______________ ______________ .

Answers

30. induced · 50
31. induced · will not
32. MPC · 7 · 7
33. less than · 1 · smaller · autonomous · real GNP

7.34

In the first round, ΔI is ______________ , which is the ______________ change in investment expenditure that starts the multiplier process. Because there is no autonomous change in consumption, in the first round ΔC is ______________ , ΔA D is ______________ , and ΔGNP is ______________ .

Table 7.1

THE MULTIPLIER EFFECT OF AN AUTONOMOUS INCREASE IN EXPENDITURE

Assume: Autonomous change in investment expenditure = 10 and MPC = 0.5

Round	Δ*C*	Δ*I*	Δ*AD*	Δ*GNP*
1	0	10.0	10.0	10.0
2	5.0	0	5.0	5.0
3	2.5	0	2.5	2.5
4	—	—	—	—
5	0.625	0	0.625	0.625
6	0.3125	0	0.3125	0.3125
.	.	.	.	.
.	.	.	.	.
.	.	.	.	.
.	.	.	.	.
Total change	10.0	10.0	20.0	20.0

7.35

The increase in real GNP that results from the autonomous increase in investment expenditure in the first round generates an ______________ increase in aggregate demand in the second round. In the second round, then, because the MPC is 0.5, ΔC is ______________ , and because we are assuming no induced changes in investment, ΔI is ______________ . As a result, ΔAD is ______________ , which causes an increase in real GNP of ______________ .

7.36

In the third round, ΔC is ______________ , ΔI is ______________ , and ΔAD is ______________ . All these changes are ______________ by the

Answers

34. 10.0 · autonomous · 0.0 · 10.0 · 10.0
35. induced · 5 · 0.0 · 5 · 5
36. 2.5 · 0.0 · 2.5 · induced

change in real GNP that resulted in the second round. In turn, they cause another increase in real GNP, of ________________ .

7.37

You can calculate for yourself and fill in the table the fourth-round effects that result from the third-round increase in real GNP. The figures in the ΔAD and ΔGNP columns are, of course, equal because for levels of GNP below potential GNP a change in aggregate demand results in an equal change in ________________ ________________ .

7.38

Because MPC is less than 1, each successive round has *(larger/smaller)* changes than the one before. As the number of rounds increases, these successive changes become closer and closer to *(0/1/10)* and become negligible.

7.39

As can be seen from the table, the sum of all the autonomous and induced changes in aggregate demand is ________________ . As a result, the total increase in real GNP is also ________________ . Because the autonomous change in aggregate demand was 10 and the total increase in real GNP was 20, the multiplier in this case is equal to ________________ .

7.40

It is no accident that the value of the multiplier in this example was 2. It resulted directly from the fact that the MPC out of real GNP was 5/10, 1/2. Suppose, for example, the MPC had been 2/3. In the second round, the increase in aggregate demand and real GNP would have been *(larger/smaller)* . As a result, if the MPC had been 2/3 instead of 1/2, the multiplier would have been *(larger/smaller)* .

Answers

36. 2.5
37. real GNP
38. smaller · 0
39. 20 · 20 · 2
40. larger · larger

7.41

If the MPC had been 2/3, you would have found that an autonomous increase in expenditure of 10 would have led to a total increase in real GNP of 30. The larger the MPC, the *(larger/smaller)* ______ will be the ______. An MPC of 2/3 yields a multiplier of 3, and, as we have seen, an MPC of 5/10, or 1/2, yields a multiplier of ______. The formula for calculating the multiplier is:

$$\text{Multiplier} = \frac{1}{1\text{-MPC}}.$$

7.42

The exact relationship between the multiplier and the marginal propensity to consume can easily be derived from what has already been discussed. You know that the final change in GNP will be equal to the ______ change and the ______ change in aggregate demand. You also know that the induced change is equal to the ______ times the final change in GNP. In symbols, then, these facts can be summarized as follows:

$$\Delta\text{GNP} = \text{autonomous } \Delta\text{AD} + \text{MPC} \times \Delta\text{GNP}$$

7.43

Subtracting "MPC X ΔGNP" from both sides of this equation results in the following equation:

ΔGNP – ______ X ______ = autonomous ΔAD.

7.44

Factoring out "ΔGNP" on the left hand side of this equation enables you to rewrite it in the following form:

______ X (1-MPC) = autonomous ΔAD.

Answers

41. larger · multiplier · 2
42. autonomous · induced (either order) · MPC
43. MPC · ΔGNP
44. ΔGNP

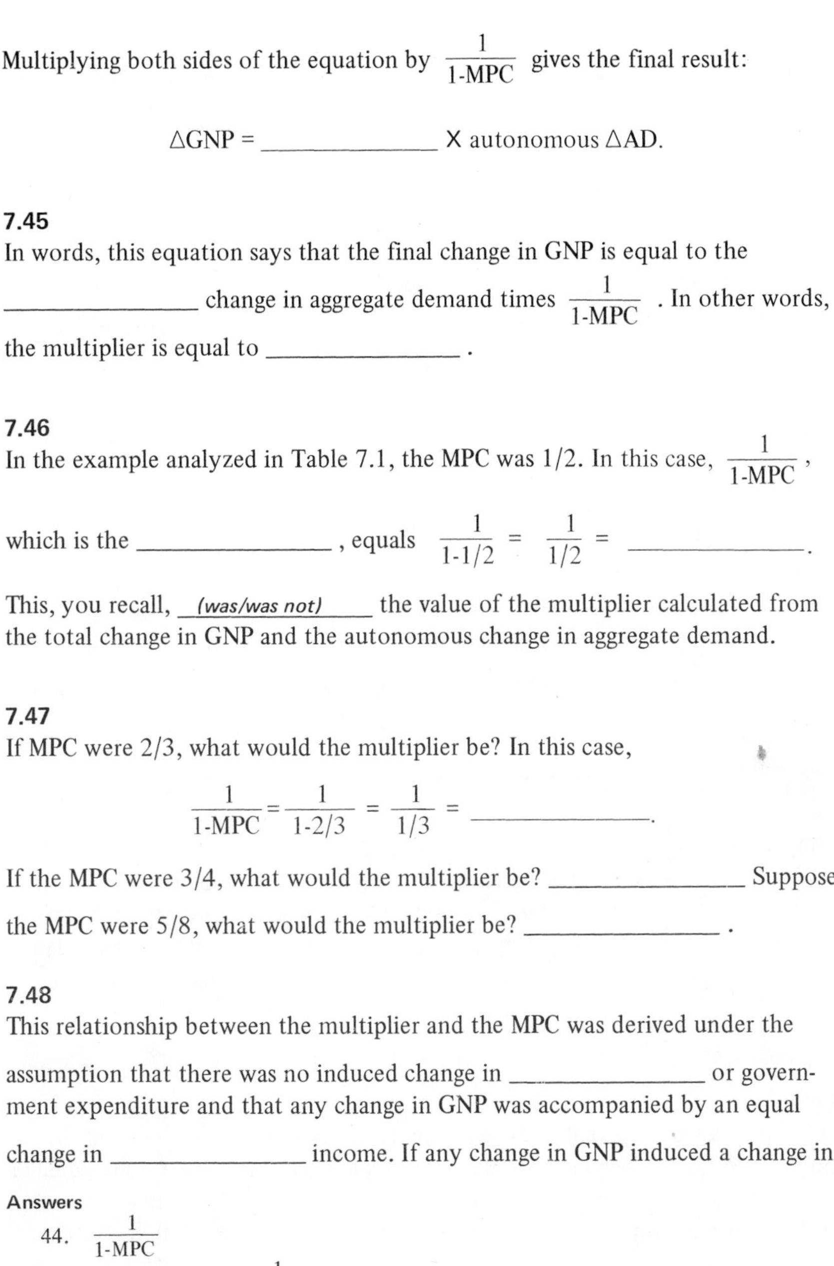

Multiplying both sides of the equation by $\frac{1}{1\text{-MPC}}$ gives the final result:

ΔGNP = ______________ X autonomous ΔAD.

7.45
In words, this equation says that the final change in GNP is equal to the ______________ change in aggregate demand times $\frac{1}{1\text{-MPC}}$. In other words, the multiplier is equal to ______________ .

7.46
In the example analyzed in Table 7.1, the MPC was 1/2. In this case, $\frac{1}{1\text{-MPC}}$, which is the ______________, equals $\frac{1}{1\text{-}1/2} = \frac{1}{1/2} =$ ______________.

This, you recall, *(was/was not)* the value of the multiplier calculated from the total change in GNP and the autonomous change in aggregate demand.

7.47
If MPC were 2/3, what would the multiplier be? In this case,

$$\frac{1}{1\text{-MPC}} = \frac{1}{1\text{-}2/3} = \frac{1}{1/3} = \text{______________}.$$

If the MPC were 3/4, what would the multiplier be? ______________ Suppose the MPC were 5/8, what would the multiplier be? ______________ .

7.48
This relationship between the multiplier and the MPC was derived under the assumption that there was no induced change in ______________ or government expenditure and that any change in GNP was accompanied by an equal change in ______________ income. If any change in GNP induced a change in

Answers

44. $\frac{1}{1\text{-MPC}}$
45. autonomous · $\frac{1}{1\text{-MPC}}$
46. multiplier · 2 · was
47. 3 · 4 · 2-2/3
48. investment · disposable

I, for example, we would also have a marginal propensity to invest (MPI) and, consequently, a *(larger/smaller)* ______ multiplier because any autonomous change in expenditure would bring about greater induced changes in expenditure. In this case, the formula for the multiplier would be:

$$\text{Multiplier} = \frac{1}{1-(\text{MPC} + \text{MPI})}.$$

In terms of our diagrams, for example Figure 7.3, the slope of the aggregate demand curve would be steeper, and the multiplier would be *(larger/smaller)* ______.

7.49

In summary, when there are unemployed resources, an ______________ increase in aggregate demand will have the effect of increasing real GNP by a *(larger/smaller)* ______ amount.

7.50

The increase in real GNP will be equal to the ______________ times the autonomous increase in aggregate demand. The size of the multiplier will depend on the ______________, which indicates how much an increase in aggregate demand will be induced by an increase in real GNP. More precisely, the multiplier will be equal to ______________.

7.51

It should be emphasized that there will be a full multiplier effect only when it is possible for real GNP to change in response to a change in aggregate demand. When there are no unemployed resources, an autonomous increase in aggregate demand *(will/will not)* ______ lead to a multiplied increase in real GNP. Instead, the increase in aggregate demand will lead to ______________.

7.52

In terms of the aggregate demand and supply diagram, there will be a full multiplier effect on real GNP from an autonomous increase in aggregate demand only if the new aggregate demand curve does not intersect the vertical portion of the aggregate supply curve. If it were to do so, part of the multiplier effect

Answers

48. larger · larger
49. autonomous · larger
50. multiplier · MPC · $\frac{1}{1\text{-MPC}}$
51. will not · inflation

would take the form of an increase in the ______________ level instead of an increase in ______________ ______________.

7.53
This can be seen in Figure 7.4, which shows an ______________ increase in aggregate demand represented by a shift in the aggregate demand curve from AD_1 to AD_2. In order for the full multiplier effect to be realized, it must be possible for the economy to reach point B. This is impossible because real GNP cannot exceed ______________ ______________, which is equal to 0P.

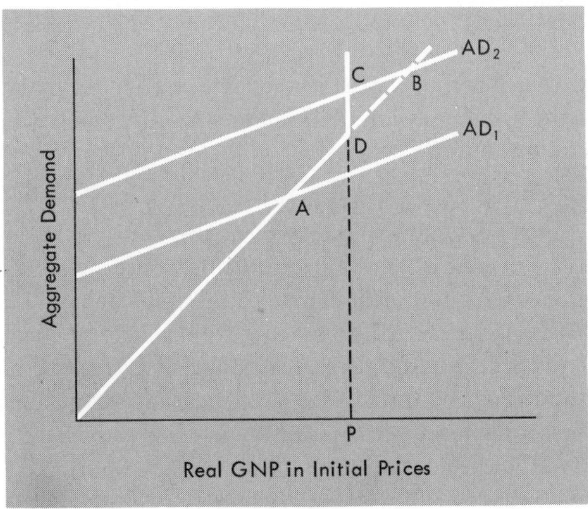

FIGURE 7.4 The absence of a full multiplier effect

7.54
As a result, instead of increasing real GNP beyond 0P, this shift in the aggregate demand curve will cause an increase in the price level. This is indicated by the ______________ gap CD.

REVIEW QUESTIONS

For all the review questions in this chapter, assume that there are no induced changes in investment expenditure and that consumption expenditure depends only on the level of disposable income.

Answers

52. price · real GNP
53. autonomous · potential GNP
54. inflationary

7.1

Last year in a certain economy, a $400 million increase in investment expenditure was accompanied by a $1 billion increase in consumer spending. Which of the following is the most likely explanation of why the consumer spending increase exceeded the investment expenditure increase?

a. In most economies, consumer expenditures in any year exceed investment expenditures.
b. Increased investment expenditures are usually accompanied by increased government expenditures.
c. Increased spending by those with higher take-home pay, caused by the increased investment expenditure, led to increased income and spending by others.
d. The increased $1 billion of consumer spending equaled the $400 million increase of investment expenditure plus the $600 million increase in government expenditure.

The multiplier process is that process by which, given unemployed resources, an exogenous increase in expenditure will generate or induce a second round of new expenditure, which in turn will induce a third round, and so on. Thus, other things remaining unchanged, an investment expenditure increase will lead to an even greater total spending increase. Although it is true that in most economies consumer expenditures in any year exceed investment expenditures, this is not the reason that increases in investment expenditure lead to increases in total spending. The correct response is c.

7.2

An autonomous increase in government expenditure must always lead to which of the following?

1. An induced increase in expenditure.
2. An increase in the price level.
   a. 1 only
   b. 2 only
   c. either 1 or 2 or both
   d. both 1 and 2

If sufficient unemployed resources exist, an increase in government expenditure will lead to an induced increase in expenditure. If there are not sufficient unemployed resources to make possible an increase in output to match the increase in government expenditure times the multiplier, an increase in government expenditure will lead to an increase in the price level because it will cause excess aggregate demand. Thus, either 1 or 2 or both must result. Both 1 and 2 need not occur simultaneously, however. The correct response is c.

7.3

If the value of the marginal propensity to consume were to increase, which of the following would result?

1. The value of the multiplier would increase.
2. Potential GNP would increase.
3. The level of investment expenditure would increase.
   a. 1 only
   b. 3 only
   c. 1 and 2 only
   d. 1 and 3 only

The value of the multiplier is $\frac{1}{1\text{-MPC}}$. Therefore, the higher the value of MPC, the higher the value of the multiplier. For example, an MPC of .5 yields a multiplier of 2, whereas an MPC of .8 yields a multiplier of 5. Neither potential GNP nor the level of expenditure depend upon the value of the MPC. The correct response is a.

7.4

The following data refer to a hypothetical economy for 1972.

$$C = \$500 \text{ million}$$
$$I = \$100 \text{ million}$$
$$G = \$100 \text{ million}$$
$$\text{Potential GNP} = \$1 \text{ billion}$$
$$\text{Value of the MPC} = \frac{2}{3}$$

Had investment expenditures been increased by $50 million and government expenditures increased by $40 million, which of the following would have occurred?

a. An increase in GNP of $90 million.
b. An increase in GNP of $270 million.
c. An increase in GNP of $540 million.
d. A rise in the price level.

With an MPC of 2/3, the value of the multiplier is 3. The increase in autonomous expenditure of $90 million ($40 million + $50 million) would lead to an increase of GNP of $90 million X 3 = $270 million. Because actual GNP equals $700, the increase of $270 is still less than potential GNP of $1 billion. Thus, there is no increase in the price level. The correct response is b.

8

Fiscal Policy

8.1

In Chapters 6 and 7, it was shown that it is possible for aggregate demand to exceed or fall short of potential GNP in initial prices. If, in the simple model, there is excess aggregate demand, the result will be ________________ . If there is insufficient aggregate demand, the result will be ________________ .

8.2

Only if aggregate demand is just equal to potential GNP in initial prices can there be ________________ ________________ without ________________ .

8.3

In Chapter 7, it was shown that in order to shift the aggregate demand curve to eliminate either excess or insufficient aggregate demand there must be an ________________ change in some component of aggregate demand.

Answers

1. inflation · unemployment
2. full employment · inflation
3. autonomous

8.4

Many factors can cause an autonomous change in aggregate demand. Unfortunately, the factors that would generate the autonomous change necessary to avoid unemployment or inflation do not always exist in a market economy. This is made evident by the data presented in Chapters 3 and 4, which show that in the United States there _*(have/have not)*___ been frequent periods of unemployment and of inflation.

8.5

Fortunately, however, it is possible for the government to take policy measures that will cause autonomous changes in aggregate demand. That is, by taking the right policy measures the government can help to avoid ______________ and ______________.

8.6

It is possible for the government to change the level of aggregate demand through *fiscal policy,* which is the general name for government expenditure and tax policies. Because the government will always be making expenditures and collecting taxes, it will always have a ______________ policy even though it may not consciously take into account its effect on the level of aggregate demand. The question here is how can ______________ policy be used to help achieve full employment without inflation?

8.7

There are several ways in which fiscal policy can be used to change the level of aggregate demand. The most obvious way is by changing government expenditure. You will recall that government expenditure includes only government purchases of ______________ and ______________. A change in government purchases of goods and services is an example of ______________ ______________.

Answers

4. have
5. inflation · unemployment (either order)
6. fiscal · fiscal
7. goods · services · fiscal policy

8.8

You will also recall that aggregate demand is the sum of consumption, investment, and ________________ expenditures. Therefore, a change in government expenditures, as long as it does not directly cause offsetting changes in private spending, is an example of how fiscal policy can be used to change the level of ________________ ________________.

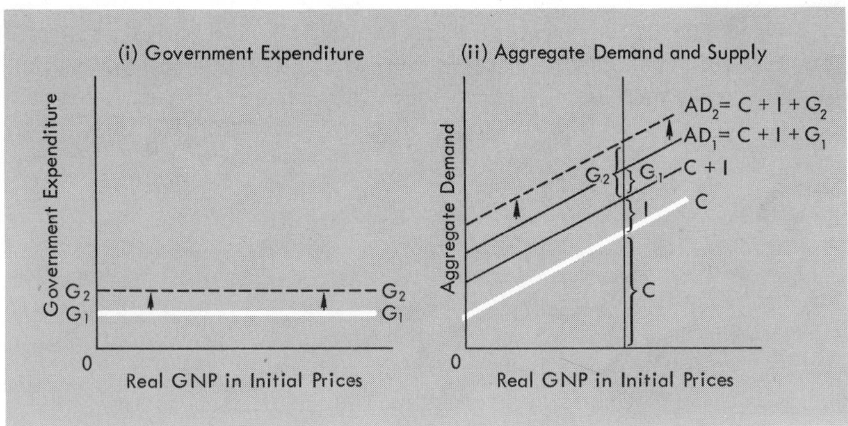

FIGURE 8.1 Government expenditure and aggregate demand

8.9

That is, given the consumption and investment functions, an increase in government expenditure will cause the ________________ ________________ curve to shift *(upward/downward)* ____ by an equal amount. This can be seen in Figure 8.1, which shows in (i) the change in government expenditure and in (ii) the effect of that change on the aggregate demand curve.

8.10

An increase in government expenditure from $0G_1$ to $0G_2$, as shown in Figure 8.1 (i), will result in an upward shift in the aggregate demand curve from __________ to ________________, as shown in Figure 8.1 (ii).

Answers

8. government · aggregate demand
9. aggregate demand · upward
10. AD_1 · AD_2

8.11

This will be the result as long as the increase in government expenditure does not cause an offsetting shift in the _______________ and _______________ functions. Is there any reason to believe that an increase in government expenditure would cause such an offsetting shift?

8.12

You might make this argument: "In order to increase government expenditure, it is necessary to raise taxes. The tax increase will reduce disposable income and, therefore, reduce consumption expenditure." This argument, however, is incorrect because it is not necessary to raise _______________ in order to increase _______________ _______________ .

8.13

It would be possible, obviously, to increase government expenditure if tax receipts were initially *(greater/less)* than government expenditure. Even if this were not true, however, by borrowing the money the government *(could/could not)* increase its expenditure without increasing taxes.

8.14

Although it is true, as will be seen later, that a change in taxes will affect consumption expenditure, it *(is/is not)* true that a change in taxes need accompany a change in government expenditure.

8.15

Thus, a fiscal policy that increases government expenditure while keeping taxes unchanged *(is/is not)* feasible. And such a policy can be expected to increase _______________ _______________ as shown in Figure 8.1.

8.16

Look now at Figure 8.2, which shows how changes in government expenditure (without a change in tax receipts) can be used to eliminate an output gap or an

Answers

11. consumption · investment(either order)
12. taxes · government expenditure
13. greater · could
14. is not
15. is · aggregate demand

inflationary gap. In Figure 8.2 (i), if the aggregate demand curve were AD_1, in equilibrium the level of aggregate demand would be ______________, real GNP would be ______________, and there would be an ______________ gap of QP.

8.17

In order to eliminate the output gap, real GNP must increase from ______________ to ______________. In order to obtain this increase without causing inflation,

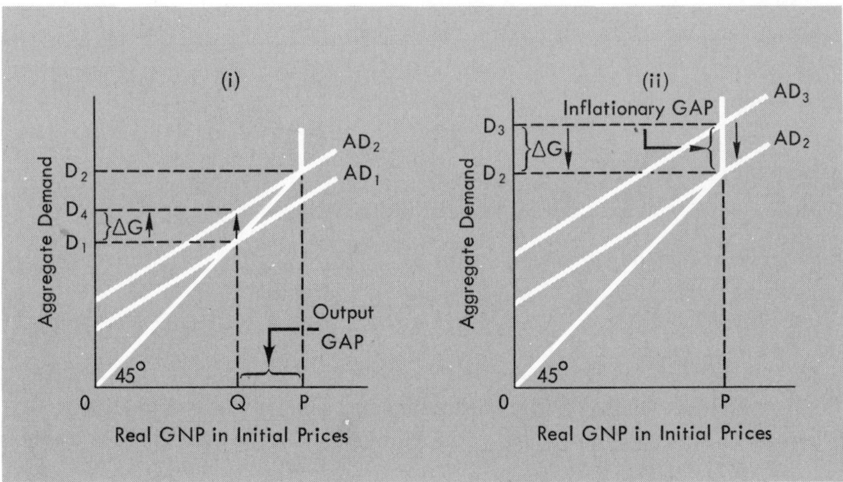

FIGURE 8.2 Government expenditure policy for full employment without inflation

it is necessary to raise the equilibrium level of aggregate demand (measuring along the vertical axis) from ______________ to ______________, that is, by the amount ______________.

8.18

In order to have a total increase in aggregate demand of D_1D_2, it is necessary to shift the aggregate demand curve from AD_1 to ______________. To have a total increase of D_1D_2 requires an autonomous increase in aggregate demand of only ______________ because of the ______________ effect.

Answers

16. $0D_1$ · $0Q$ · output
17. $0Q$ · $0P$ · $0D_1$ · $0D_2$ · D_1D_2
18. AD_2 · D_1D_4 · multiplier

8.19

In this example, then, an increase in government expenditure of the amount $D_1 D_4$ (with tax receipts unchanged) will result in a total increase in aggregate demand of ______________ and the elimination of the ______________ gap without ______________ .

8.20

Suppose that initially the aggregate demand curve had been AD_3, as shown in Figure 8.2 (ii), instead of AD_1. In this case, the economy would be at full employment but would also be confronted with an ______________ gap. It would be possible for the government to eliminate this gap by *(increasing/decreasing)* its expenditure.

8.21

If government expenditure were reduced by the amount ______________ , the aggregate demand curve would shift to ______________ , and the economy could have full employment *(with/without)* inflation.

8.22

If government expenditure were reduced by an amount greater than $D_2 D_3$, the inflationary gap *(would/would not)* be eliminated. At the same time, however, such a policy would cause ______________ .

8.23

What these examples indicate is that in our simple model of the economy changes in government expenditure *(can/cannot)* be used to move the economy toward full employment without inflation, because a change in government expenditure will shift the ______________-______________ curve.

Answers

19. $D_1 D_2$ · output · inflation
20. inflationary · decreasing
21. $D_2 D_3$ · AD_2 · without
22. would · unemployment
23. can · aggregate demand

8.24
As was indicated earlier, to change government expenditure is not the only way in which fiscal policy can be used to eliminate either excess or insufficient

______________ ______________ . An alternative to a change in government expenditure is a change in taxes.

8.25
The exact effect of a change in taxes on the economy depends in part on the type of tax that is changed. For example, a change in corporate profits taxes will affect the rate of return that businesses earn on capital goods and can, therefore, be expected to affect ______________ expenditure.

8.26
Changes in taxes of different types, although they vary in many ways, will have similar effects on aggregate demand. For this reason, only one type of tax change will be analyzed in detail. Consider the effects of a change in the personal income tax on aggregate demand. You will recall that the income consumers have available to spend is called ______________ income. It is equal to GNP minus retained business income *(plus/minus)* transfer payments *(plus/minus)* taxes.

8.27
Given the level of GNP, then, an increase in income taxes will *(increase/decrease)* disposable income, and a decrease in income taxes will *(increase/decrease)* disposable income.

8.28
You will also recall that disposable income appears to be the basic determinant of ______________ expenditure. When disposable income increases, ______________ expenditure ______________ .

Answers

24. aggregate demand
25. investment
26. disposable · plus · minus
27. decrease · increase
28. consumption · consumption · increases

8.29

Thus, given the level of real GNP, because an increase in taxes will *(increase/decrease)* disposable income, it will also cause *(an increase/a decrease)* in consumption expenditure.

8.30

Similarly, a decrease in taxes will cause *(an increase/a decrease)* in consumption expenditure.

8.31

The immediate result of a change in taxes, then, is an *(induced/autonomous)* change in consumption expenditure, and therefore in aggregate demand as well.

It is an ______________ change because it is brought about by a factor *other* than a change in real GNP.

8.32

Like any other autonomous change in aggregate demand, an autonomous change brought about by tax policy will lead to ______________ changes in aggregate demand as well. That is, tax changes will cause autonomous changes in aggregate demand that will have a ______________ effect.

8.33

These results can be seen in Figures 8.3 and 8.4, which show the effects of tax reduction on disposable income, consumption expenditure, aggregate demand, and real GNP. Look at Figure 8.3 (i). This diagram shows consumption expenditure as a function of ______________ ______________.

8.34

Suppose that real GNP is 0Q, as shown in Figure 8.3 (ii), and that with initial taxes disposable income is $0Y_1$. Then, consumption expenditure will be

______________.

Answers

29. decrease · a decrease
30. an increase
31. autonomous · autonomous
32. induced · multiplier
33. disposable income
34. $0C_1$

8.35
Now suppose there is a tax cut in the amount of $Y_1 Y_2$. Then, at the same level of GNP 0Q, disposable income will increase to ______________, and consumption will increase to ______________.

8.36
You will recall that the proportion of any increase in disposable income that will be spent by consumers is called the marginal propensity to consume, or MPC. Thus, the increase in consumption expenditure, $C_1 C_2$, will be equal to the ______________ times the change in disposable income, $Y_1 Y_2$.

8.37
For a given level of real GNP, then, a decrease in taxes of $Y_1 Y_2$ will increase ______________ ______________ by the same amount, as is shown in Figure 8.3 (i). This will result in a *(shift in/movement along)* the consumption function in terms of disposable income and an increase in consumption expenditure equal to the ______________ times the tax cut.

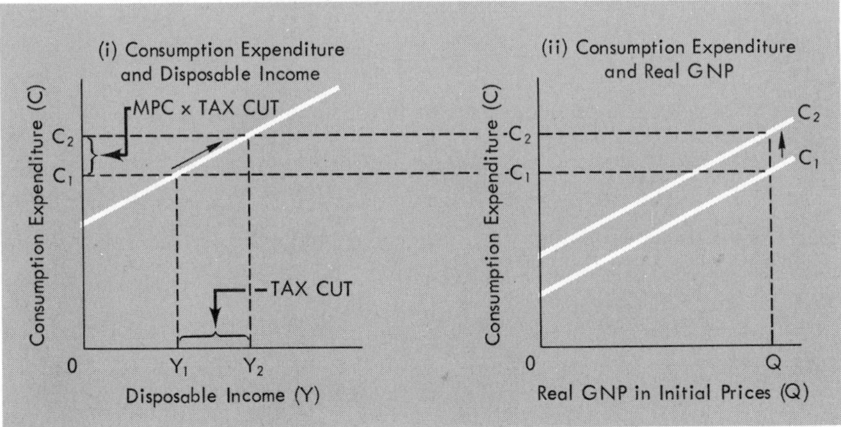

FIGURE 8.3 The consumption function and tax reduction

Answers

35. $0Y_2$ · $0C_2$
36. MPC
37. disposable income · movement along · MPC

8.38

Look now at Figure 8.3 (ii). This diagram shows consumption expenditure as a function of ______________ ______________ . As you know from the analysis of Figure 8.3 (i), with taxes at their initial level, when real GNP is 0Q, disposable income will be $0Y_1$, and consumption expenditure will be ______________ . In Figure 8.3 (ii), this is indicated by the consumption function ______________ .

8.39

After the tax cut, however, when real GNP is 0Q, disposable income will be ______________ , and consumption expenditure will be ______________ . That is, for the same real GNP, consumption expenditure will now be *(higher/lower)* than before the tax cut.

8.40

At any level of real GNP, consumption expenditure would be higher after the tax cut than before. As a result, the effect of the tax cut will be an *(induced/autonomous)* increase in consumption expenditure and, in Figure 8.3 (ii), an upward *(shift in/movement along)* the consumption function.

8.41

The amount of this autonomous increase in consumption expenditure will, of course, be equal to the ______________ times the decrease in taxes. For this reason, the amount of the shift in the consumption function (in terms of real GNP) is also equal to the ______________ times the decrease in ______________ .

8.42

The effect of tax reduction on aggregate demand and real GNP can be seen in Figure 8.4. This diagram shows how a change in taxes can be used to eliminate unemployment without causing inflation. With a consumption function of C_1

Answers

38. real GNP · $0C_1$ · C_1
39. $0Y_2$ · $0C_2$ · higher
40. autonomous · shift in
41. MPC · MPC · taxes

and the corresponding aggregate demand curve of AD_1, the equilibrium level of real GNP will be ________________. Without policy action by the government, the result will be *(unemployment/inflation)* and an ________________ gap of QP.

8.43

In this situation, a policy of *(increasing/decreasing)* taxes would be appropriate. *(An increase/A decrease)* in taxes would shift the consumption function up by an amount equal to the ________________ times the tax *(increase/decrease)*.

8.44

Such a policy action is depicted in Figure 8.4. Both the consumption function and the aggregate demand curve shift up by the MPC times the tax increase. This

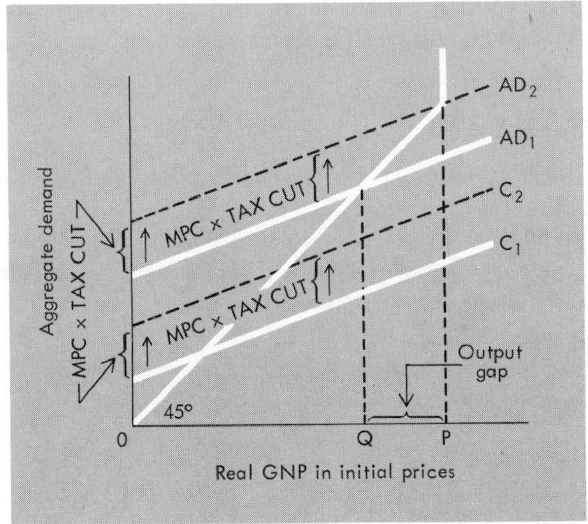

FIGURE 8.4 Tax reduction to achieve full employment

will lead to further ________________ increases in aggregate demand and a total increase in real GNP equal to the ________________ times the initial autonomous increase in aggregate demand.

Answers

42. 0Q · unemployment · output
43. decreasing · A decrease · MPC · decrease
44. induced · multiplier

8.45

A smaller tax cut would have reduced, but would not have completely eliminated, the output gap. A larger tax cut *(would/would not)* ________ have eliminated unemployment but at the same time would have caused ________ .

8.46

Thus, you have seen that tax policy as well as expenditure policy, if used properly, is a powerful tool for maintaining the economy at ________ ________ without ________ .

8.47

In addition to changes in government expenditure and taxes, fiscal policy to influence aggregate demand can take the form of changes in transfer payments. You will remember that most transfer payments are transfers of income from the ________ to ________ . An increase in transfer payments, therefore, will *(increase/decrease)* ________ disposable income.

8.48

Furthermore, an increase in transfer payments will have the same effect on disposable income as *(an increase/a decrease)* ________ in taxes of an equal amount. For this reason, policy action that takes the form of an increase in transfer payments *(will/will not)* ________ have the same effect on aggregate demand as a decrease in taxes of the same amount. The same applies, of course, for a decrease in transfer payments and *(an increase/a decrease)* ________ in taxes.

8.49

For example, a tax increase of $10 billion or a decrease in transfer payments of $10 billion would each result in an autonomous *(increase/decrease)* ________ in consumption expenditure equal to the ________ times $10 billion.

Answers

45. would · inflation
46. full employment · inflation
47. government · consumers · increase
48. a decrease · will · an increase
49. decrease · MPC

8.50

In summary, then, given our simple model, if it appears that there will be either inflation or unemployment, the government *(could/could not)* ______ prevent it from occurring by using appropriate fiscal policy.

8.51

If inflation threatens, it would be appropriate for the government to *(increase/decrease)* ______ taxes, *(increase/decrease)* ______ transfer payments, or *(increase/decrease)* ______ government expenditure. Or the government could undertake any combination of these three actions.

8.52

In this case, the effect of any or all of these policies would be to *(increase/decrease)* ______ aggregate demand, thereby reducing the ______ gap.

8.53

The government would have to use caution in taking any of these policy actions, for too great a decrease in aggregate demand would create an ______ gap and cause ______ .

8.54

If unemployment is the problem, the government would reduce it by doing any or all of the following: *(increase/decrease)* ______ taxes; *(increase/decrease)* ______ transfer payments; *(increase/decrease)* ______ government expenditure.

8.55

Again, these changes would have to be made in the proper amount. If they were too great, ______ ______ would increase by too great an amount, and ______ would result.

Answers

50. could
51. increase · decrease · decrease
52. decrease · inflationary
53. output · unemployment
54. decrease · increase · increase
55. aggregate demand · inflation

8.56

The arguments used to justify such policy measures to fight inflation or unemployment make good common sense in the real world. Put simply, inflation results when, at initial prices, buyers want to purchase *(more/less)* output than can be produced and bid up prices. Unemployment results when, at initial prices, buyers want to purchase *(more/less)* output than can be produced; because the price level tends to be inflexible in a downward direction, producers *(increase/decrease)* production and employment.

8.57

Thus, when there is a threat of inflation, fiscal policy should be designed to *(increase/decrease)* total expenditure. When faced with unemployment, the government should take action to *(increase/decrease)* total expenditure.

8.58

Changes in total expenditure can be brought about either by changes in public spending or by changes in private spending. If the decision is made to change public spending, then obviously the government can change its own expenditure directly. If it is decided to change private spending, the government can change consumption or investment expenditure indirectly by changing

_______________ and _______________ _______________.

8.59

Despite the fact that the use of fiscal policy to stabilize the economy makes good sense, there has been strong opposition to it on the grounds that it sometimes requires the government to have a *budget deficit.* Whenever government expenditure plus transfer payments is greater than taxes, there is a _______________ in the government's budget.

8.60

For example, if government expenditure is $60 billion, transfer payments are $30 billion, and taxes are $70 billion, there is a budget _______________ of $ _______________ billion.

Answers

56. more · less · decrease
57. decrease · increase
58. taxes · transfer payments
59. deficit
60. deficit · 20

8.61

Suppose that initially the government's budget is balanced. That is, suppose government expenditure plus transfer payments equals ________________. Suppose also that at the same time there is unemployment. If the government were to increase government expenditure or transfer payments or decrease taxes to eliminate unemployment, the budget *(would/would not)* be a budget deficit.

8.62

In this case, fiscal policy *(increases/decreases)* the deficit from zero to a positive level. If initially there had been a budget deficit, then an appropriate change in government expenditure, transfer payments, or taxes would *(increase/decrease)* the budget deficit to an even higher level.

8.63

In these two situations, then, fiscal policy to eliminate unemployment increases the ________________. Is there any reason why fiscal policy should not be used, as in these two cases, when it increases the budget deficit?

8.64

One argument against using fiscal policy to eliminate unemployment if it will increase the deficit is that budget deficits cause inflation. As you know, inflation results when ________________ ________________ exceeds ________________ ________________ in initial prices. You also know that an increase in the deficit–whether it comes about through an increase in government expenditure or transfer payments or a reduction in taxes–will *(increase/decrease)* aggregate demand.

8.65

But an increase in aggregate demand brought about by an increase in the deficit *(must/need not)* result in a level of aggregate demand that is greater than potential GNP in initial prices. In particular, if there is unemployment in the economy, aggregate demand initially will be *(greater/less)* than potential GNP in initial prices.

Answers

61. taxes · would
62. increases · increase
63. deficit
64. aggregate demand · potential GNP · increase
65. need not · less

8.66

In this situation, in terms of the simple model outlined in Chapters 6 and 7, the increase in aggregate demand brought about by an increase in the deficit will simply bring aggregate demand up to the level of potential GNP in initial prices. The increase in aggregate demand will result in an increase in *(output/prices)* .

Instead of causing inflation, the increase in the deficit will reduce ________ .

8.67

It is true, of course, that if the economy were initially at full employment without inflation, an increase in the deficit would cause ________ . In this case, the increase in the deficit would raise ________ ________ above potential GNP in initial prices.

8.68

What can be said, in summary, about the relationship between budget deficits and inflation? First, the mere fact that in a particular year there is a budget deficit *does not* by itself mean that there will be either inflation or full employment. That is, it *(is/is not)* possible to have unemployment if there is a budget deficit, and it *(is/is not)* necessary that there be inflation if there is a budget deficit.

8.69

If there is both unemployment and a budget deficit, it would be possible to reduce unemployment by *(increasing/decreasing)* the deficit. This could be accomplished by increasing government expenditure or transfer payments or by decreasing taxes.

8.70

If there is price stability and no unemployment along with a budget deficit, the deficit should be *(increased/decreased/unchanged)* .

Answers

66. output · unemployment
67. inflation · aggregate demand
68. is · is not
69. increasing
70. unchanged

8.71

If there is both inflation and a budget deficit, the deficit should be *(increased/decreased)* ________ by decreasing government expenditure or transfer payments or by ________ taxes.

8.72

The budget is not restricted to being either balanced or having a deficit. It is also possible for there to be a budget *surplus.* This will occur when government expenditure plus transfer payments is *(greater/less)* ________ than taxes.

8.73

It is possible for there to be either inflation or unemployment when there is a budget surplus. If there is inflation with a budget surplus, the government should have had a *(larger/smaller)* ________ surplus to have avoided inflation. If there is unemployment with a budget surplus, the surplus should have been *(larger/smaller)* ________ to have avoided unemployment.

8.74

What matters is not whether there is a surplus, deficit, or budget balance, but how the actual condition of the budget compares with the ideal condition that would ensure full employment with price stability. If the actual budget differs from the ideal budget, then government expenditure, transfer payments, or taxes *(should/should not)* ________ be changed to attain the ideal. In *(some/all)* ________ situations, the ideal budget will be balanced. In others, it will show a deficit. In still others, it will show a surplus.

8.75

In order to have a balance between aggregate demand and real GNP at initial prices, it *(is/is not)* ________ always necessary to have a balanced budget.

8.76

Thus, budget deficits *(do/do not)* ________ automatically cause inflation. Therefore, fear of inflation *(is/is not)* ________ always necessary to have a balanced budget.

Answers

71. decreased · increasing
72. less
73. larger · smaller
74. should · some
75. is not
76. do not · is not

8.77

Concern with inflation has not been the only basis for opposition to the use of _______________ policy to attain full employment without inflation when rational policy requires a budget deficit. Objections to having a budget deficit are sometimes based on the belief that a large *national debt* is harmful.

8.78

The national debt is the amount owed by the federal government to people and institutions from which it has borrowed money. When the government has a budget deficit, government expenditure plus transfer payments is *(greater/less)* than taxes, and it is necessary for the government to borrow to make up the difference. This increases the national _______________.

8.79

In Figure 8.5, the amount of the national debt is shown for the period 1929–1971. Those years in which the national debt increased must be years in which there was a budget _______________. Figure 8.5 shows that since 1929 the national debt has *(increased/decreased)* substantially, especially during the World War II period.

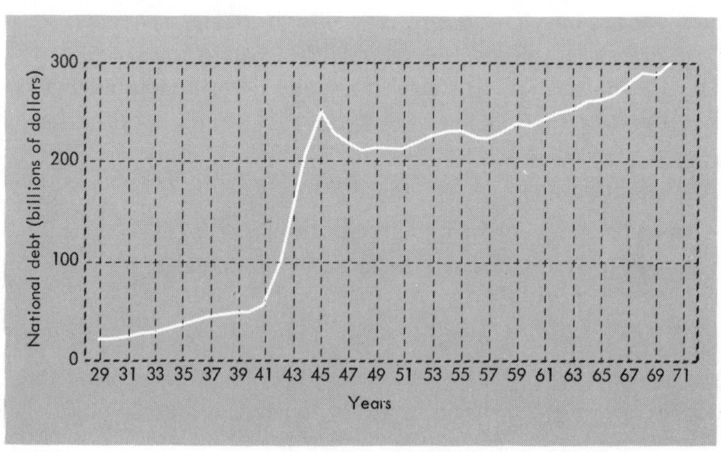

FIGURE 8.5 The national debt, 1929–1971 (billions of dollars)

Answers

77. fiscal
78. greater · debt
79. deficit · increased

8.80

Is it harmful to have a large national debt? Many believe that it is and make the following argument:

"If a businessman continues to spend more than his income, he will eventually be in financial trouble. Some day, his debt will reach a level that is beyond his means to repay, and he will be forced into bankruptcy. Not only will the businessman be out of business but his creditors will be left holding worthless debt. If the national debt becomes too great, the result will be a bankrupt government and impoverished bondholders. If a businessman must live within his means, so must the government." This argument implies that if the national debt becomes too large, the government *(will/will not)* be able to repay the holders of government bonds. It also implies that the government *(should/should not)* be run like a business.

8.81

Both these implications are incorrect, however. First, the government has very special powers that ensure its ability to repay loans. These powers are the authority to tax and the authority to create new money. That is, the government *(will/will not)* be able to pay back its debt because it can always obtain the necessary money by collecting ______________ or by creating new ______________.

8.82

A business has neither of these powers, and for this reason the amount it can safely borrow depends on the income it can earn. Government borrowing, however, is not limited by the size of government earnings because the government has the authority to ______________ and to create new ______________.

8.83

Second, the government should not be run like a business. Its objectives *(are/are not)* to make as large a profit as possible, *(not/but)* to perform certain services for the people it represents. Many useful services performed by the government, such as carrying out justice or conducting foreign policy, *(are/are not)* profit-making activities.

Answers

80. will not · should
81. will · taxes · money
82. tax · money
83. are not · but · are not

8.84

It is generally accepted that the government should take action to prevent unemployment and inflation that would otherwise occur. If this sometimes requires running a budget deficit, the government *(should/should not)* be prevented from doing so just because that runs contrary to normal business financial practice.

8.85

There is another reason that people have been opposed to policy actions that increase the national debt. The following argument is frequently made:

"Suppose the government makes an expenditure and pays for it by borrowing money instead of collecting taxes. Then, the present generation will obtain the benefits of that expenditure without having to pay for it. When the debt must be repaid, the government will have to collect taxes, with the result that a future generation will have to pay for the expenditure of the present generation."

This argument states that when government expenditure is financed by issuing debt instead of collecting taxes, the burden of paying for it is borne by *(the present/a future)* generation.

8.86

To evaluate this argument, consider the real economic cost (that is, opportunity cost) of any government expenditure. It is the private output (for example, automobiles, factories, and so on) that could have been produced with the

________________ used to produce the output purchased by the government, that is, the opportunity cost. Consequently, in deciding whether to make any additional expenditure, the government should evaluate the benefits to society to determine whether they exceed this cost.

8.87

Suppose that a given additional expenditure is considered worth undertaking. Then, the question arises as to how it should be financed. Should the government increase taxes or should it borrow to obtain the money to make its purchases? The answer to this question depends in part on whether the economy is at full employment. If it is at full employment, the government can obtain more goods only if private purchases of goods *(increase/decrease)* by the same amount. If GNP is equal to its potential, an increase in one type of ex-

Answers

84. should not
85. a future
86. resources
87. decrease

penditure (for example, government) can occur only if there is a ______________ in some other type (for example, consumption or investment).

8.88

If there is unemployment, however, it is possible to increase government purchases without reducing real consumption or investment expenditure because the output purchased by the government could be produced with the otherwise ______________ resources.

8.89

In the case in which there is full employment, if the government wants to avoid inflation, it must choose a method of financing its expenditure that *(increases/decreases)* private expenditure by the same amount. One way to do this would be to raise taxes, by enough to reduce disposable income and thereby reduce ______________ expenditure. In this way, *(a future/the present)* generation would pay for the government expenditure by foregoing some consumption.

8.90

In the case in which there is unemployment, it would be possible and desirable to increase government expenditure without reducing private expenditure. The result, according to our model, would be a decrease in *(unemployment/inflation)* without any ______________. If there were many unemployed resources, it would *not* be appropriate to finance the expenditure with taxes because to do so would restrain private ______________ expenditure.

8.91

If the expenditure were financed by borrowing, the multiplier effect of an autonomous increase in expenditure could cause *(an increase/a decrease)* in consumption expenditure. If the resulting total aggregate demand did not exceed potential GNP, the consequences would be all to the good: total output, government expenditure, and private expenditure would all ______________, unemployment would ______________, and there would be no excess aggregate demand to cause inflation.

Answers

87. decrease
88. unemployed
89. decreases · consumption · the present
90. unemployment · inflation · consumption or investment
91. an increase · increase · decrease

8.92

If we can assume that in the absence of the additional government expenditure the unemployed resources would have remained idle, then in a sense neither the present nor a future generation would have to pay for the output purchased by the government. It would be produced by ______________ that would otherwise be wasted in ______________ .

8.93

Thus, we can see that when there is full employment, it makes sense to avoid inflation by financing additional government expenditure through ___________ . And, when there is unemployment, it is appropriate for the government to pay for additional purchases by borrowing and consequently reduce ___________ .

8.94

But what about the government debt that is accumulated when the government finances its expenditure by borrowing? Does it not place a burden on future generations? Clearly, in the example we presented above, the answer is no. In that case, the output purchased by the government did not replace output of private capital goods. Because the capital stock was not made lower than it otherwise would have been, the goods and services available for future consumers were not diminished. Instead, the output purchased by government was produced by resources that would otherwise have been ______________ . Consequently, in this case, the government expenditure *(does/does not)* diminish the resources that will be left to future generations and does not impose a burden on future generations.

8.95

If and when it appears desirable to pay off the government debt, future tax payers will contribute the money to buy back the government bonds from future bondholders. This will be a transfer from the American people to the American people and will not involve any loss of ______________ for the U.S. economy, although there would be some redistribution of wealth.

Answers

92. resources · unemployment
93. taxes · unemployment
94. unemployed · does not
95. resources (output)

8.96

You have seen in this chapter how _______________ policy can be used to stabilize the economy. Sometimes sound policy will involve a budget deficit. Other times, it may require a budget surplus. Neither course of action taken in appropriate circumstances will serve to impoverish future generations, but can substantially benefit the present generation by helping to assure full employment without inflation.

REVIEW QUESTIONS

8.1

In the United States in 1961, there was high unemployment; in 1968 there was full employment. In both years, the government increased expenditure for goods and services. With respect to the increase in government expenditure, which of the following is correct?

a. It is more likely that the expenditure would be possible without a sacrifice of private goods in the year of high unemployment.
b. It is more likely that the expenditure would be possible without a sacrifice of private goods in the year of full employment.
c. The expenditure is likely to influence prices more than real output in the year of high unemployment.
d. The expenditure is likely to influence real output more than prices in the year of full employment.

When an economy is operating at full employment, an increase in the flow of goods and services to one group of purchasers (for example, government) is possible only if the flow of goods and services to all other groups of purchasers (consumers and firms) is reduced. When unemployed resources exist, however, increased spending by one group can, through the multiplier process, lead to additional expenditure by others, the employment of idle resources, and a larger total flow of goods and services. In other words, a decrease in unemployment occurs that leads to a higher national output. For this reason, when sufficient resources are idle, additional government expenditure does not cause a sacrifice of private goods. On the contrary, it causes an increase in the flow of private goods and services as well as an increase in government output. The correct response is a.

Answers

96. fiscal

8.2

A government has estimated the difference between its actual and full employment national income to be $2 billion and has decided to increase its expenditure on domestically produced goods by that amount, but to keep tax rates and interest rates unchanged.

Assuming the government wants to get to full employment with as little inflation as possible and also assuming that consumers spend only part of increases in their income,

a. this policy is not sufficiently expansionary.
b. this policy is about right.
c. this policy is too expansionary.
d. which of the above is correct cannot be determined from the above information.

The multiplier process is that process by which, given unemployed resources, an exogenous increase in expenditure will generate or induce a second round of new expenditure, which in turn will induce a third round, and so on. If the economy is operating at full employment, however (or if full employment is reached before the multiplier process is complete), the increase in aggregate demand will generate higher prices, not additional output. Thus, the $2 billion increase in government expenditure is too expansionary. If, for example, the value of the multiplier is 5, an increase in government expenditure, *certeris paribus,* of $400,000 million will induce an additional $1.6 billion expenditure, which is just the amount of total additional output required to yield full employment without excess aggregate demand. The correct response is c.

8.3

There is considerable unemployment in the economy. The government is proposing to finance an $800 million increase in expenditure for goods and services with an $800 million increase in income taxes. If other things were unchanged, and if consumers always spend 90 percent of their after-tax income, such a scheme would:

a. raise national income.
b. leave national income unchanged.
c. lower national income by $800 million.
d. lower national income by $720 million.

Initially, the government expenditure increase of $800 million would be only partially offset by a $720 million decrease in consumption expenditure (90 percent of the $800 million tax increase). As a result, the proposed changes in government expenditure and taxes would cause an exogenous increase in expenditure of $80 million, which would induce further increase in expenditure and national income of $720 million, that is, the total increase in national income would be $800 million. Thus, the expansionary effect of the increase in government expenditure outweighs the deflationary effect of the increase in taxes. The correct response is a.

8.4

Which of the following would be likely to result if the government increased its spending without increasing its tax receipts during a period of full employment?

a. Inflation and a decrease in the national debt.
b. Inflation and an increase in the national debt.
c. Recession and a decrease in the national debt.
d. Recession and an increase in the national debt.

At full employment, an increase in real expenditure by the government would be possible if there was a corresponding decrease in real expenditure by consumers and/or firms. If no corresponding decrease took place and given capacity is fixed, an attempt by the government to increase real expenditure would lead to excess aggregate demand and a rise in the price level. In addition, this increase in money expenditure by the government, holding tax receipts constant, will cause an increase in the national debt. The correct response is b.

9

Investment Expenditure and the Interest Rate

9.1

Just as the government can carry out fiscal policies that lead to changes in private consumption expenditure, it can also influence investment expenditure. Although consumption expenditure is made to satisfy consumers' wants directly, investment expenditure is made to earn a profit. When a business makes investment expenditure, it hopes to increase its capacity to produce and sell output and thereby earn a ______________ . Unless it is expected that an expenditure for a particular capital good (for example, a new machine or building) would yield a ______________ , that expenditure will not be made.

9.2

In order to be profitable, the capital good investment must return enough money after all other expenses to more than cover the cost of buying the capital good. For example, if an oil well costs $100,000 to construct and run and yields only $90,000 worth of oil before it runs dry, it *(would/would not)* ______________ be profitable to make that expenditure. If it yielded $105,000 worth of oil, there would be a return over cost of $ ______________ .

Answers

1. profit · profit
2. would not · 5,000

9.3

The return over cost of an investment is usually calculated in the same way as for a savings account or government bond. For example, a government bond that costs $18.25 and yields $25.00 after eight years is usually described as a bond that has a *rate of interest* of 4 percent per year. That is, if you invest $18.25 and earn 4 percent in interest per year, after eight years your original investment plus the ______________ will be worth $ ______________.

9.4

A similar concept can be applied to investment in capital goods. In this case, the average annual return over cost is called the *rate of return.* The yearly percentage return over cost earned by an investment is the ______________ of ______________. For the oil well, if it costs $100,000 and yields $105,000 after one year and nothing thereafter, it is an investment with a rate of return of ______________ percent per year.

9.5

In order to be worth buying, a capital good must return more than just its purchase price. It must also return as much as any other asset in which the money could have been invested. That is, it is not sufficient that an investment have a positive ______________ of ______________. It must have a rate of return that is as high as the rate that can be earned on any other asset. Otherwise, it *(would/would not)* be better to buy the other asset.

9.6

For example, suppose the oil well has a rate of return of 5 percent per year. This means that it *(does/does not)* have a large enough return to cover its cost. But this *(does/does not)* indicate by itself whether the investment is worth making.

9.7

Suppose that you could earn 6 percent per year in interest on a savings deposit in your bank. This means that after one year an initial deposit of

Answers

3. interest · 25.00
4. rate · return · 5
5. rate · return · would
6. does · does not

$100,000 would be worth $ ______________. Clearly, with this opportunity available, you *(would/would not)* ______ invest in the oil well.

9.8

In general, businesses have the alternative of investing in capital goods or investing in financial assets such as government bonds or bank accounts. A business will find it profitable to invest in any capital good that yields a higher

______________ of ______________ than the rate of interest that can be earned on financial assets, making allowances for differences in risk.

9.9

The lower the rate of interest is, the *(more/less)* ______ investment expenditure will be worth making, other things remaining equal.

9.10

Thus, a major factor in determining the level of investment expenditure is the

______________ of ______________ against which the rate of return is compared in deciding whether any investment expenditure is worth making.

9.11

The greater the rate of interest, the *(greater/smaller)* ______ will be the amount of investment expenditure worth making, other things remaining equal.

9.12

This relationship between the rate of interest and investment is shown in terms of a rate of return function in Figure 9.1. In this diagram, both the rate of

interest and the rate of return are measured along the ______________ axis,

and investment expenditure is measured along the ______________ axis.

Answers

7. 106,000 · would not
8. rate · return
9. more
10. rate · interest
11. smaller
12. vertical · horizontal

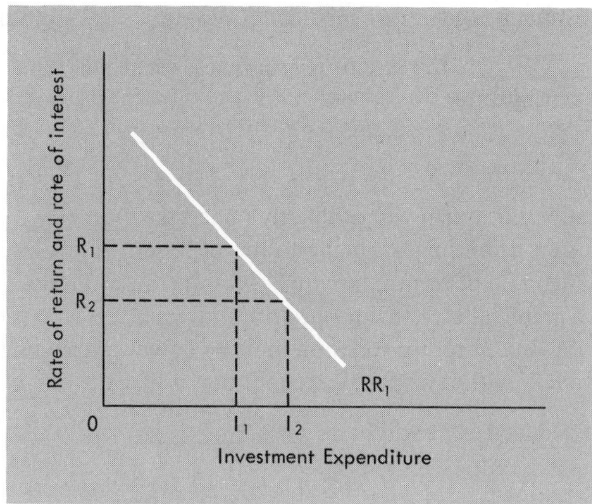

FIGURE 9.1 The rate of return function

9.13

Curve RR is an example of the ________________ of ________________ function. This function shows, for different levels of investment expenditure, the rate of return on an extra dollar of investment expenditure. Curve RR, for example, shows that if investment expenditure were $0I_1$, the ________________ of ________________ on an extra dollar of investment would be ______________.

9.14

As can be seen in Figure 9.1, the rate of return function slopes *(upward/downward)* from left to right. Thus, the greater the amount of investment expenditure, the *(higher/lower)* the rate of return that can be earned on the last dollar of investment expenditure.

9.15

Suppose you were to rank all possible investment expenditures in decreasing order in terms of the rate of return on each. That is, put first those investment expenditures that will yield a rate of return of 20 percent or more, then those yielding 15 percent or more, then those of 10 percent or more, and so on. Then, you can see that the lower the rate of return, the *(greater/smaller)* the

Answers

13. rate · return · rate · return · $0R_1$
14. downward · lower
15. greater

amount of investment expenditure included. Conversely, the more that is invested, the ______________ the rate of return that is earned on the last dollar of investment expenditure.

9.16

Profit-motivated businessmen will ordinarily undertake *(first/last)* ____ those investment projects promising the highest rates of return. A few investments will promise a high rate of return, more will promise lower rates of return. Thus, if you plot on a graph all investment opportunities against the rates of return they promise, the rate of return function must be downward sloping to the right. For curve RR, with investment expenditure of $0I_2$, the rate of return on an extra dollar of investment will be ______________ .

9.17

From the rate of return function, it is possible to tell how much investment expenditure businessmen would want to make at different rates of interest. As long as the rate of return on an investment project is *(higher/lower)* ____ than the rate of interest, it will be worth undertaking. Investment expenditure will be made up to the point where *(no/some)* ____ projects will remain that have a rate of return higher than the rate of interest. At this point, the rate of return will be *(greater than/equal to/less than)* ____ the rate of interest.

9.18

In Figure 9.1, for example, given the rate of return function RR, if the rate of interest were $0R_1$, businesses would want to make no more and no less investment expenditure than ______________ . At the lower rate of interest $0R_2$, investment expenditure would be the *(greater/smaller)* ____ amount ______________ .

9.19

Thus, in terms of the aggregate demand and supply model, a change in the rate of interest will cause an ______________ change in investment expenditure. As you have seen, like any other autonomous change in investment expenditure, it will appear as a *(shift in/movement along)* ____ the investment function.

Answers

15. lower
16. first · $0R_2$
17. higher · no · equal to
18. $0I_1$ · greater · $0I_2$
19. autonomous · shift in

9.20

Because a change in the rate of interest will cause a shift in the investment function, it will also cause a shift in the ____________ ____________ curve. As a result, a change in aggregate demand due to a change in the rate of interest *(can/cannot)* be expected to have an impact similar to autonomous changes in aggregate demand caused by other factors.

9.21

Specifically, an increase in the rate of interest will cause an autonomous *(increase/decrease)* in investment expenditure and aggregate demand. Unless there were an inflationary gap to begin with, the increase in the interest rate would have the effect of *(increasing/decreasing)* unemployment. If there were an inflationary gap to begin with, the increase in the interest rate would *(widen/narrow)* the inflationary gap.

9.22

A reduction in the rate of interest, of course, will have the opposite effect. It will cause *(an increase/a decrease)* in aggregate demand and will tend to *(widen/narrow)* the output gap or *(widen/narrow)* the inflationary gap, depending on the situation.

9.23

This can be seen in terms of Figure 9.2. The rate of return function for the economy is shown in Figure 9.2 (i). This function indicates the amount of investment expenditure there will be for different rates of ____________. With the rate of return function RR, at a rate of interest $0R_1$, investment expenditure will be ____________.

9.24

In Figure 9.2 (ii), curve I_1 is the investment function when the rate of interest is $0R_1$. I_1 shows, given the rate of interest $0R_1$, the ____________ ____________ that will be made at different levels of ____________

Answers

20. aggregate demand · can
21. decrease · increasing · narrow
22. an increase · narrow · widen
23. interest · $0I_1$
24. investment expenditure · real

________________. With the investment function I_1, when real GNP is 0Q, investment expenditure will be ________________.

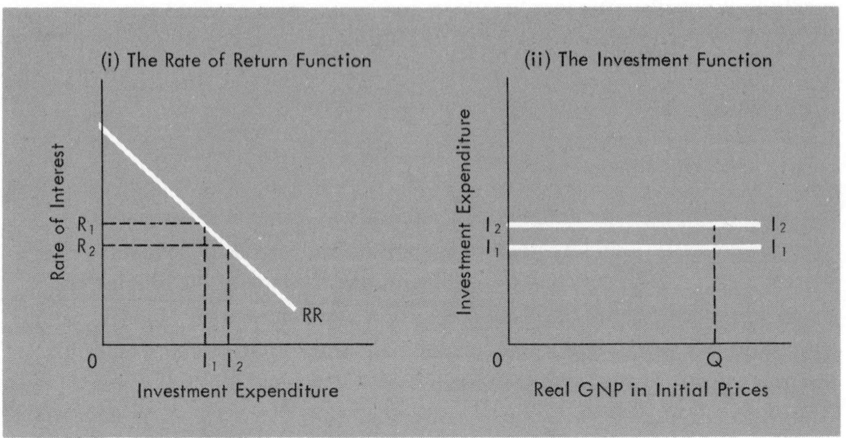

FIGURE 9.2 The rate of interest and investment expenditure

9.25

For a real GNP of 0Q, if the rate of interest changes, there will result a *(shift in/movement along)* the RR curve in Figure 9.2 (i). At an interest rate of $0R_2$, investment expenditure will be ________________.

9.26

At the same time, a change in the rate of interest from $0R_1$ to $0R_2$ will result in a *(shift in/movement along)* the investment function in Figure 9.2 (ii). At a rate of interest of $0R_2$, the investment function will be I_2 and, at a real GNP of 0Q, investment expenditure will be ________________.

9.27

Thus, in terms of the aggregate demand and supply model, a change in the rate of interest will cause an ________________ change in investment expenditure. As you have seen, like any other autonomous change in investment expenditure, it will appear as a *(shift in/movement along)* the investment function.

Answers

24. GNP · $0I_1$
25. movement along · $0I_2$
26. shift in · $0I_2$
27. autonomous · shift in

9.28

Because a change in the rate of interest will cause a shift in the investment function, it will also cause a shift in the ________ ________ curve. As a result, a change in aggregate demand due to a change in the rate of interest *(can/cannot)* be expected to have an impact similar to autonomous changes in aggregate demand caused by other factors.

9.29

Specifically, an increase in the rate of interest will cause an autonomous *(increase/decrease)* in investment expenditure and aggregate demand. Unless there were an inflationary gap to begin with, the increase in the interest rate would have the effect of *(increasing/decreasing)* unemployment. If there were an inflationary gap to begin with, the increase in the interest rate would *(widen/narrow)* the inflationary gap.

9.30

A reduction in the rate of interest, of course, will have the opposite effect. It will cause *(an increase/a decrease)* in aggregate demand and will tend to *(widen/narrow)* the output gap or *(widen/narrow)* the inflationary gap, depending on the situation.

9.31

A change in the rate of interest can also cause an autonomous change in consumption expenditure. You will recall from Chapter 2 that certain expenditures, such as purchases of automobiles, furniture, and so on, made by households are in large part ________ expenditures but are counted as ________ expenditures in the GNP.

9.32

Considerations similar to those that underly the investment decisions of businesses influence the expenditure by households for consumers' durable goods. When considering the purchase of an automobile, for example, it will make sense to buy only if the benefit derived from the car is *(greater/less)*

Answers

28. aggregate demand · can
29. decrease · increasing · narrow
30. an increase · narrow · widen
31. investment · consumption
32. greater

than the _______________ of the car. Also, the benefit must be enough greater than the cost to cover the _______________ that can be earned by buying a financial asset like a bond or a savings account.

9.33

Consequently, the higher the rate of interest, the *(higher/lower)* will be expenditure for consumers' durable goods and the *(higher/lower)* will be aggregate demand. A change in the rate of interest can affect aggregate demand by causing changes in both _______________ and _______________ expenditure.

9.34

The reason for analyzing the effect of a change in the rate of interest is not only that it will have an important effect on the economy but also that government policy can change the rate of interest. Thus, by taking appropriate action to change the rate of interest, the _______________ can change the level of aggregate demand to move the economy toward full employment without inflation.

9.35

In order to understand how the government can influence the rate of interest, it is necessary to understand how the rate of interest is determined in a market economy. You will recall that interest is the payment, over and above repayment of the amount borrowed, that *(borrowers/lenders)* must make to *(borrowers/lenders)*.

9.36

The percentage of an amount borrowed for a year that must be paid in interest is called the _______________ of interest. This means that the rate of interest is the number of cents that must be paid for borrowing one dollar for a year. Just as the number of cents per loaf is the price of bread, the rate of interest is the _______________ of borrowing money for a year.

Answers

32. cost · interest
33. lower · lower · consumption · investment (either order)
34. government
35. borrowers · lenders
36. rate · price

9.37

For example, if you were to borrow $100 for two years, the rate of interest would indicate how much you would have to pay each year for the use of that money. If the rate of interest were 8 percent, you would have to pay

_______________ cents per dollar each year. Your total interest for two years

would be $ _______________ . In this example, the 8 percent rate of interest

is the _______________ of borrowing money for a year.

9.38

Just as there are markets in which goods and services can be bought and sold, there is a market in which money can be borrowed and loaned. This market is called the money market. If you were to borrow money from a bank, for

example, you would be making a transaction in the _______________

_______________ . The price you would have to pay is the _______________

of _______________ .

9.39

In the U.S. economy, there are actually many types of loans. For example, there are mortgages, corporate bonds, personal loans, and many others. These differ in terms of the purpose for which the money is borrowed, type of security offered the lender, the time for which the loan is made, and so on. In general, just as different cuts of meat have different prices, different types of

loans will have different prices or _______________ of _______________ .
Thus, if you were to look in the financial section of the newspaper for the current rate of interest, you would find *(just one rate/many rates)* of interest.

9.40

Although a study of differences among types of loans is very important for some purposes, it is not essential for an understanding of how rates of interest are determined or how government policy can change investment expenditure by influencing the money market. To simplify, therefore, it will be assumed here that there is only one kind of loan and, therefore, only one rate of interest. In other words, the following discussion will *(explain/ignore)* differences

Answers

37. 8 · 16 · price
38. money market · rate · interest
39. rates · interest · many rates
40. ignore

among types of loans and rates of interest because those differences *(are/are not)* ____ important to an understanding of how government policy can influence investment expenditure through the money market.

9.41

When a loan is made, a *note*, or promise to pay, which obligates the borrower to pay the lender the amount borrowed plus ____________, is sold to the lender in the money market. This note is sometimes called a security. For example, when a business borrows money to build a factory, it sells a ____________ that commits it to repay the loan with interest. When a bank makes a loan, it *(buys/sells)* ____ a note, or ____________. (Such a security is often called a *bond.*)

9.42

If you own a security that was previously issued by a borrower, it is often possible to sell it in the money market. If you need money for some purpose, you can obtain it either by issuing and selling a new ____________ or by selling an existing ____________ that you own.

Thus, the money market is a market in which both new and previously issued ____________ are bought and sold. (Sometimes existing securities cannot be sold again in the money market. Promissory notes given to banks in return for bank loans are an example of nonmarketable securities. Bonds are usually marketable securities.)

9.43

Securities are sold to obtain ____________. Usually, new securities are issued to enable the borrower to spend *(more/less)* ____ than his current income for goods and services. For example, when a family buys a house, the cost of the house is usually more than the family's yearly income. By selling a new ____________, that is, by borrowing money, it is possible to obtain the money necessary to buy the house. (This type of security is usually called a *mortgage.*)

Answers

40. are not
41. interest · security · buys · security
42. security · security · securities
43. money · more · security

9.44

To take another example, you will recall that when the government runs a budget ________________ , it must borrow money by issuing and selling ________________ in the money market.

9.45

A person, business, or government who has issued securities that are still outstanding is called a *debtor.* At any point in time, the amount owed by a ________________ will not be simply the amount borrowed in the current period. Rather, it will be the total amount of securities issued by the ________________ that have not yet been repaid.

9.46

For example, in 1971 the federal government's budget deficit was $23 billion, which means that during 1971 it had to sell, in addition to any new securities issued to replace existing securities that came due during the year, $ ________________ billion worth of securities. At the end of 1971, the total outstanding debt of the federal government was $23 billion *(larger/smaller)* ________ than it was at the end of 1970. The total outstanding debt at the end of 1971, $326 billion, was much larger than $23 billion because it included *(all/no)* ________ securities issued in previous years that had not yet been repaid.

9.47

Similarly, for persons and business, any time money is borrowed to spend more for goods and services than is available from current income, new ____________ must be issued and sold, and the total outstanding debt must *(increase/decrease)* ________ .

9.48

For every debtor who has securities outstanding, there must be a creditor who owns those securities. For example, if you owned a security that had been issued by the American Telephone and Telegraph Corporation, you would be a ________________ , and AT&T would be a ________________ .

Answers

44. deficit · securities
45. debtor · debtor
46. 23 · larger · all
47. securities · increase
48. creditor · debtor

9.49

In the same way, every security is both an asset and a liability at the same time. To creditors, securities are ________________, and to debtors they are ________________.

9.50

How do creditors obtain the funds to acquire securities? You will recall from Chapter 2 that, for the economy as a whole, income must be equal to expenditure. As has just been discussed, however, income and expenditure *(must/need not)* be equal for every individual consumer, business, or government.

9.51

Although it *(is/is not)* possible for total expenditure to be different from total income for the economy as a whole, this *(is/is not)* possible for an individual consumer, business, or government, by their selling ________________ in the money market.

9.52

But, because total income must equal total expenditure, for every borrower who spends more than his income there must be a ________________ who spends *(more/less)* than his income. This is reflected in the fact that every time a security is sold by someone, it must be ________________ by someone else.

9.53

Creditors, then, are consumers, businesses, or governments who have spent *(more/less)* on goods and services than they have received in income and have accumulated financial *(assets/liabilities)*.

Answers

49. assets · liabilities
50. need not
51. is not · is · securities
52. lender · less · bought
53. less · assets

9.54

At the same time, debtors are consumers, businesses, or governments who have spent ___*(more/less)*___ on goods and services than they have received in income and have accumulated financial ___*(assets/liabilities)*___.

9.55

The assets of ________________ and the liabilities of ________________ are the same financial securities. They are the means by which those who save part of their income make it available to those who want to spend more than their income.

9.56

The price paid by debtors to creditors for the temporary use of the creditors' unspent income is the ________________ of ________________. In the next chapter, it will be explained how the rate of interest adjusts to make the amount of securities that debtors have issued equal to the amount creditors want to hold.

REVIEW QUESTIONS

9.1

Which of the following would be an appropriate statement to make about a person who is a creditor?

1. He has used only part of his present and past income to purchase goods and services.
2. He has acquired financial assets.
3. He has loaned part of his present or past income to a debtor.
   a. 1 and 3 only
   b. 1, 2, and 3
   c. 2 and 3 only
   d. 3 only

Answers

54. more · liabilities
55. creditors · debtors
56. rate · interest

A creditor is a person who owns an asset that is the IOU of another person. To acquire that asset, a creditor must have used part of his present or past income instead of spending it on a good or service. Also, the asset is a financial asset. Finally, the act of buying an IOU from another person is equivalent to making a loan to him. The correct response is b.

9.2

The reason why a decline in the rate of interest will, other factors unchanged, lead to an increase in investment expenditure is that the decline in the rate of interest will

a. increase the rate of return on investment.
b. reduce consumption expenditure.
c. increase the number of investment projects with a rate of return greater than the rate of interest.
d. cause creditors to want to lend more to investors.

Businesses that are profit maximizers will undertake investments for which the rate of return is greater than the rate of interest. When the rate of interest declines, some projects that previously were unprofitable will become worth undertaking, and investment expenditure will increase. A decline in the rate of interest will neither increase the rate of return nor directly reduce consumption expenditure nor cause creditors to want to lend more. The correct response is c.

9.3

Dramatic increases in expenditure for the war abroad are likely to cause serious inflation at home unless the government restricts the growth of aggregate private demand. Suppose the government is considering either increasing interest rates or increasing personal income taxes. Which policy would have the lesser adverse effect on growth of potential GNP?

a. The increase in interest rates, because this will restrict consumption expenditures more than investment expenditure.
b. The increase in interest rates, because this will restrict investment expenditure more than consumption expenditure.
c. The increase in personal income taxes, because this will restrict consumption expenditure more than investment expenditure.
d. Each policy will have the same effect on economic growth–that is, no effect, because economic growth is independent of government actions.

Given that aggregate demand has increased due to the increase in government expenditure to the point where there is an inflationary gap, it will be necessary to reduce some other component of aggregate demand to avoid inflation. If this is done by reducing investment expenditure, then the amount by which the capital stock will increase in the current period will be reduced, and, consequently, the growth in potential GNP will be reduced. Because interest rates primarily influence consumption expenditure, growth in potential GNP will be less adversely affected by increasing income taxes. The correct answer is c.

9.4

"The basic theory of national income determination makes clear that fiscal policy is the main factor determining the level of aggregate demand and, consequently, the level of unemployment and the rate of inflation. All the discussion in the newspapers about changes in interest rates may be of significance to bond holders, but it is of no relevance to the important developments in the economy." Do you agree or disagree with this statement and why?

a. Agree, because the key factors determining the level of GNP are autonomous changes in aggregate demand.
b. Agree, because the interest rate is not a component of aggregate demand.
c. Disagree, because the interest rate is a reflection of how well the economy is achieving its potential.
d. Disagree, because the interest rate is an important determinant of aggregate demand.

The fact that aggregate demand is the key variable in determining the state of the economy does not imply either that fiscal policy is the main factor determining the level of aggregate demand or that the interest rate is not an important determinant of aggregate demand. The interest rate is one factor that influences the level of investment expenditure and, consequently, the level of aggregate demand. The correct answer is d.

10

The Demand for and Supply of Money

10.1
In Chapter 9, it was noted that some consumers, businesses, or governments have not spent all of the income they have earned and have accumulated *(assets/liabilities)*______ in the form of securities. Such persons are called *(debtors/creditors)*______ .

10.2
Securities, however, are not the only asset that creditors can hold. It is also possible to hold wealth in the form of *money*. That is, creditors have a choice between holding their assets in the form of ______________ or __________ .

10.3
Obviously, given their total wealth, the more securities creditors hold, the *(more/less)*______ money they will be able to hold. Thus, if a creditor wants to increase his holdings of securities, he must reduce his holdings of ____________ .

Answers

1. assets · creditors
2. securities · money (either order)
3. less · money

10.4

Money, like a security, is an asset. Unlike a security, however, money does not earn interest. Why is anyone willing to hold money, which yields no interest, when it is possible to hold ________ which do yield interest? There are two basic reasons why asset holders are willing to give up ________ by holding money instead of securities.

10.5

It has already been noted that money is an ________. In Chapter 3, it was noted that money is whatever is generally accepted in *payment* for goods and services. Money, then, is an ________ that is a generally accepted means for making ________.

10.6

Because money is the usual means of payment, if a person holds only securities, it will be necessary for him to sell a security to obtain money each time he wants to purchase a real commodity. This would be fine if securities could be sold at any time and without cost. Then it would be possible to earn as *(much/little)* interest as possible from your financial assets *(without/but not without)* interfering with your shopping needs.

10.7

Unfortunately, securities cannot be sold at any time. In the evening and on weekends, it would be difficult to sell a security and, therefore, it *(would/would not)* be difficult to do any desired shopping. Also, it is not costless to sell securities. There are brokers' fees, visits and phone calls to your broker, and the time required to make such arrangements. Thus, in order to earn the maximum interest from your securities by holding only securities, it *(is/is not)* necessary to incur certain costs connected with selling securities when money is needed to make purchases.

Answers

4. securities · interest
5. asset · asset · payment
6. much · without
7. would · is

10.8

It is possible to avoid these selling costs by holding some ________________ . In fact, most persons and businesses do hold money just to avoid these selling ________________ . Thus, one reason for holding money is to meet transactions needs for money without having to pay the unwanted costs of selling securities each time you want to buy a commodity. Holding money for this reason is called the *transactions demand* for money.

10.9

If there were no costs of time, effort, or money associated with selling securities, there would be no ________________ demand for money. Because there are such costs and most people consider them not worth paying, there is a ________________ ________________ for money.

10.10

A second reason for holding money stems from the fact that the market value of securities can change over time. Money, on the other hand, will always have a fixed value in dollar terms. That is, the dollar value of ________________ can change over time, but the dollar value of ________________ remains fixed.

10.11

Compared to money, securities are riskier financial assets because the amount that a security will sell for in the money market fluctuates over time as the eagerness of other to buy it changes. A dollar is always a dollar, but a security for which you paid $100 may be worth only $90 next month. If you hold securities instead on money, you earn more ________________ on your holdings, but you also must accept greater *(risk/safety)* .

10.12

Most asset holders choose to hold at least part of their wealth in the form of money in order to avoid the *(risk/interest)* that comes with holding securities.

Answers

8. money · costs
9. transactions · transactions demand
10. securities · money
11. interest · risk
12. risk

That is, most people hold money as a precaution against the possibility of a *(rise/fall)* ________ in the market value of securities.

10.13

Many people hold money for precautionary purposes to make sure that at least part of their wealth is not lost due to declines in the value of securities in the money market. If some people did not consider the *(safety/risk)* ________ gained from holding some of their wealth in money to outweigh the ________ lost from not holding all of their financial assets in securities, they would not hold money for ________ purposes.

10.14

In addition to holding money for precautionary purposes, people hold money for speculative purposes. If an asset holder became convinced that the market value of securities was going to fall, he obviously *(would/would not)* ________ want to hold securities and would prefer to hold ________ instead. That is, asset holders will want to hold money for speculative purposes if they expect the market value of securities to *(rise/fall)* ________ .

10.15

The holding of money for precautionary and speculative purposes is called the *asset demand* for money. Holding money to facilitate the purchase of goods and services is called the ________ demand. And the holding of money for precautionary or speculative reasons is called the ________ demand.

10.16

The two basic reasons for holding money, then, are:

a. the avoidance of selling costs to obtain money to make purchases when desired, which gives rise to the ________ demand, and
b. the avoidance of the risk attached to holding securities or an expectation that the market value of securities will fall, which give rise to the ________ demand.

Answers

12. fall
13. safety · interest · precautionary
14. would not · money · fall
15. transactions · asset
16. transactions · asset

10.17

These reasons explain why asset holders are willing to forego some of the ________________ that could be earned if they held only securities and no money.

10.18

How much money will the public be willing to hold? The riskiness and costs of selling securities make asset holders willing to give up some ________________. How much risk and selling costs asset holders will avoid by holding money will depend on how much ________________ they must give up to do so.

10.19

If interest rates are high, then they must give up *(a lot of/little)* ______ interest to hold money and avoid a given amount of risk and selling costs. When interest rates are high, therefore, asset holders can be expected to hold *(more/less)* ______ money than when interest rates are low, other things being equal.

10.20

When interest rates are relatively low, asset holders will hold *(more/less)* ______ money because they have to give up less ________________ to avoid the risk and selling costs that come with holding securities.

10.21

This can be seen in Figure 10.1, where line L is the demand curve for money. This demand curve shows the quantity of money that asset holders will want to hold at different rates of interest. Because at high interest rates it is necessary to give up a relatively large amount of ________________ to avoid the ____________ and ________________ ________________ from holding securities, asset holders will want to hold *(more/less)* ______ money than at low interest rates. For this reason, the demand curve for money slopes *(upward/downward)* ______ from left to right.

Answers

17. interest
18. interest · interest
19. a lot of · less
20. more · interest
21. interest · risk · selling costs · less · downward

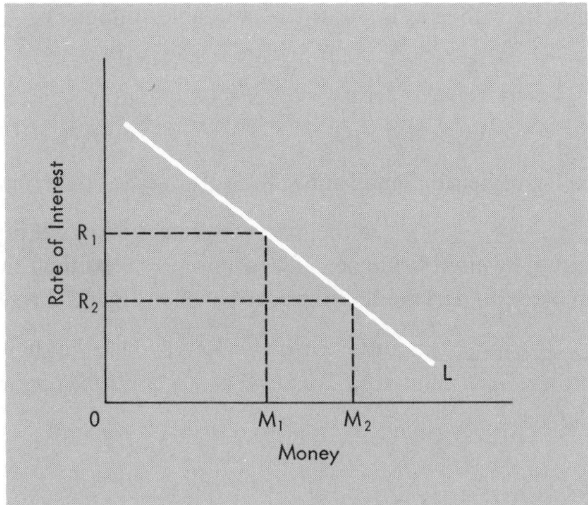

FIGURE 10.1 The demand for money

10.22

For example, at the rate of interest $0R_1$, asset holders want to hold an amount of money equal to _______________. At the rate of interest $0R_2$, they will want to hold more of their financial assets in _______________ and less in _______________. In this case, the quantity of money demanded will be _______________.

10.23

What are the conditions under which the money market is in equilibrium? Equilibrium exists when there is no tendency for changes in any of the relevant variables, such as the quantities demanded and supplied and the rate of interest. For example, if forces exist that tend to raise the rate of interest, then the money market cannot be in _______________. Only when all of the variables in a market "come to rest" can there be _______________.

10.24

In any market, the basic condition for equilibrium is equality between the quantities demanded and supplied. This means in the case of the money market

Answers

22. $0M_1$ · money · securities · $0M_2$
23. equilibrium · equilibrium

that asset holders are willing to hold just the available amounts of ____________ and ____________.

10.25

Why is the equality of demand and supply for both money and securities a condition for ____________ in the money market? Suppose, for example, that for a given rate of interest the demand for money is less than the supply. This means that asset holders are holding more of their financial assets in the form of ____________ than they wish to. (Remember, that here the question under consideration is how total financial assets are to be divided between money and securities.)

10.26

Because the only alternative financial asset is securities, when the demand for money is less than the supply this also means that asset holders wish that some of their assets that take the form of ____________ were ____________ instead. Thus, to say that there is an excess demand for money is equivalent to saying that there is an excess ____________ of securities.

10.27

In this situation, some asset holders will try to adjust their holdings by using the excess holdings of ____________ to buy ____________ from other asset holders. In order to induce them to sell their securities, these buyers must offer to pay more for the securities than they were worth initially.

10.28

Suppose that a typical security was issued in the amount of $100 at an interest rate of 4 percent. This means that the holder would receive $ ____________ in interest per year. Suppose that someone were to buy that security from its holder for $120. The second owner would still get $ ____________ per year in interest from the debtor, which means that he would earn a *(higher/lower)* ____ rate of interest because he paid more for the security. The

Answers

24. money · securities (either order)
25. equilibrium · money
26. money · securities · supply
27. money · securities
28. 4 · 4 · lower

second owner would earn $ ______________ per year on a financial investment of $ ______________ .

10.29

Thus, when asset holders bid up the value of securities in the money market, at the same time they also bid *(up/down)* ______ the rate of interest. When there is an excess supply of money, asset holders in trying to acquire securities with their excess money holdings will *(increase/decrease)* ______ the market value of securities and drive *(up/down)* ______ the interest rate.

10.30

This makes common sense when you consider new securities issues. When asset holders at the initial rate of interest would like to hold less money and more securities than they have, they are likely to offer a *(higher/lower)* ______ rate of interest to debtors to induce them to supply them with more securities. Thus, an excess supply of money, which means an excess demand for securities, will result in a *(rise/fall)* ______ in the rate of interest. (Remember, again, that here the only question being considered is how total financial assets are to be divided between money and securities.)

10.31

Because the demand for money curve slopes *(downward/upward)* ______ from left to right, a decline in the interest rate will *(increase/decrease)* ______ the quantity of money demanded.

10.32

Thus, if there is an excess supply of money, the rate of interest will *(rise/fall)* ______ and the quantity of money demanded will *(increase/decrease)* ______ .

10.33

The rate of interest will continue to fall until the resulting increase in demand *(doubles/eliminates)* ______ the excess supply. At this point, equilibrium will be attained in the ______________ market.

Answers

28. 4 · 120
29. down · increase · down
30. lower · fall
31. downward · increase
32. fall · increase
33. eliminates · money

10.34

The reverse, of course, holds true when there is an excess demand for money. In this case, asset holders will try to sell unwanted securities and bid their value in the market *(up/down)* ______ and the rate of interest *(up/down)* ______ until equilibrium is established.

10.35

This can be seen in terms of Figure 10.2, in which line L is the demand curve for money and line M shows the supply of money. The fact that M is shown as a *(horizontal/vertical)* ______ line implies that the amount of money outstanding *(does/does not)* ______ change when the rate of interest changes.

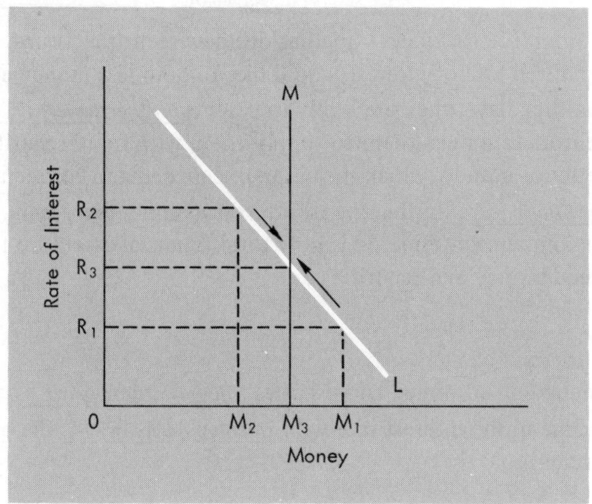

FIGURE 10.2 The supply and demand for money

10.36

If the rate of interest were $0R_1$ in Figure 10.2, the amount of money demanded would be ______, which is *(greater/less)* ______ than the amount of money supplied. At this rate of interest, the money market *(will/will not)* ______ be in equilibrium, and the rate of interest will tend to *(rise/fall)* ______.

10.37

At the rate of interest $0R_2$, there will be an excess *(supply of/demand for)* ______ money, and the rate of interest will tend to *(rise/fall)* ______.

Answers

34. down · up
35. vertical · does not
36. $0M_1$ · greater · will not · rise
37. supply of · fall

10.38

Only if the rate of interest is ______________ will the money market be in ______________. That is, at a rate of interest of $0R_3$ the amount of money supplied and demanded *(will/will not)* be equal, and there will be *(a/no)* tendency for the rate of interest to change.

10.39

At the same rate of interest, $0R_3$, the supply and demand for securities must also be equal. When the quantities of money supplied and demanded are equal, it means that asset holders are not trying to use their money holdings to acquire more securities than are in existence nor are they trying to convert any of their securities into money. That is, when the amounts of money supplied and demanded are equal, the money market is in ______________ because the supply and demand for ______________ are also equal and there is no tendency for the rate of interest to change. Thus, it *(is/is not)* necessary to analyze the supply and demand curves for securities to identify the equilibrium rate of interest.

10.40

You have now seen how the rate of interest is determined in the economy. The rate that will prevail in the money market is the rate by which the quantities of money ______________ and ______________ are equal. Only at that rate will the money market be in ______________.

10.41

In summary, money is held for two basic reasons. One is to avoid the cost of converting securities to money whenever a purchase of real commodity is made. The holding of money for this reason is called the ______________ demand for money. The other is to avoid some of the risk that comes with holding securities or to avoid losses if you expect the market value of securities to fall. The holding of money because it is safer than securities is called the ______________ demand for money.

Answers

38. $0R_3$ · equilibrium · will · no
39. equilibrium · securities · is not
40. supplied · demanded (either order) · equilibrium
41. transactions · asset

10.42

The rate of ________________ will adjust to make the quantity of money demanded equal to the quantity ________________ . But what determines the supply of money?

10.43

Money is the generally accepted means of ________________ . In the United States, currency and checks drawn on bank deposits are generally accepted as means of payment and are, therefore, called ________________ .

10.44

When you go to the store, it is possible to purchase goods and services either by exchanging ________________ for them or by writing a check against your ________________ in the bank. Because currency and bank deposits can generally be used to purchase commodities, they are called ________________ .

10.45

Currency and bank deposits are ________________ because they are generally accepted as means of ________________ . To the holders of currency and bank deposits, they are *(assets/liabilities)* ________ .

10.46

Consider currency first. If you look at a five-dollar bill, for example, you will see that it is a *Federal Reserve Note.* This is because it is issued by the Federal Reserve, which is the central, or government, bank in the United States. Just as ordinary persons issue securities, the central bank issues Federal Reserve Notes. For this reason, currency, or ________________ ________________ Notes, are *(assets/liabilities)* ________ of the Federal Reserve.

Answers

42. interest · supplied
43. payment · money
44. currency · deposit · money
45. money · payment · assets
46. Federal Reserve · liabilities

10.47

Federal Reserve Notes are a very special liability, because by law they can be used to settle any debt. This is indicated on the Federal Reserve Note where it says, "This note is legal tender for all debts public and private." That is, currency is generally accepted as a means of payment because by law it *(must/need not)* be accepted as such. Thus, even though it is a ____________ of the Federal Reserve, the only way a holder of currency will be repaid is with other Federal Reserve Notes. Of course, because currency *(must/may)* be accepted as means of payment in the United States, there is no reason to ask for other money in exchange.

10.48

Bank deposits are similar to currency. Currency is the liability of the ____________ ____________, which is the central bank; a bank deposit is the liability of *commercial banks.* If you have a bank deposit, that means that *(you owe the bank/the bank owes you)* the amount deposited.

10.49

Persons usually hold bank deposits to avoid the risk of loss or theft of currency, and because bank checks are a convenient means of payment. They are willing to hold bank deposits instead of currency because a check written on a bank deposit, like currency, *(is/is not)* generally accepted as a means of payment. Unlike currency, however, there is no law that requires a person to accept a check written on a bank deposit. But, if you can show that you have a bank deposit, your check will usually be accepted as a means of payment because everyone knows that the ____________ will convert the check without delay into currency if this is desired.

10.50

Thus, bank deposits are ____________ because they are generally accepted as a means of payment. Bank deposits are the *(assets/liabilities)* of commercial banks, which are willing and able to convert the deposits into ____________ without delay.

Answers

47. must · liability · must
48. Federal Reserve · the bank owes you
49. is · bank
50. money · liabilities · currency

10.51

How does money come into existence? Through a complicated procedure, which is not important for this discussion, the Federal Reserve may issue currency when it buys securities in the money market. When it buys securities, the Federal Reserve may pay for them in effect by issuing currency, or ________________ ________________ ________________, which by law are means of ____________. These, of course, become *(assets/liabilities)* ________ of their holder and *(assets/liabilities)* ________ of the Federal Reserve.

10.52

For example, suppose that the Federal Reserve's total asset holdings consisted of $100 billion in securities that had been purchased in the money market and paid for with Federal Reserve Notes. If that were the case, the balance sheet of the Federal Reserve, which shows its assets and liabilities, would look like this:

Assets	*Liabilities*
Securities . . . $100 billion	Federal Reserve Notes . . . $100 billion

That is, the $100 billion in securities would be the ________________ and the $100 billion in currency would be the ________________ of the Federal Reserve. It would also mean that the amount of currency circulating in the economy would be $ ________________ billion. That is, all the liabilities of the Federal Reserve would be held as ________________ by consumers, businesses, and other government agencies.

10.53

Now, if the Federal Reserve decided to purchase $10 billion more in securities with Federal Reserve Notes, after this purchase its balance sheet would appear as follows (fill in the amounts):

Assets	*Liabilities*
Securities . . . $____ billion	Federal Reserve Notes . . . $____ billion

Now the public's asset holdings would include $10 billion more in *(currency/securities)* ________ and $10 billion less in *(currency/securities)* ________.

Answers

51. Federal Reserve Notes · payment · assets · liabilities
52. assets · liabilities · 100 · assets
53. 110 · 110 · currency · securities

10.54
Thus, currency comes into existence when the Federal Reserve purchases

________________ from the public in the money market and pays for them

with ______________ ______________ ______________ .

10.55
Bank deposits come into existence in much the same way. The most familiar way is when someone deposits currency in the bank and gets a bank deposit in return. In this case, one form of ______________ is being exchanged for another. When a bank exchanges bank deposits for currency, money *(is/is not)* created. Nonbank-asset holders are simply exchanging one kind of ____________ for another.

10.56
Bank deposits, however, can be created in another way. When the bank makes a loan (that is, buys a ______________), it usually gives the lender a new bank deposit. That is, when banks buy securities they usually pay for them with

______________ ______________ .

10.57
Thus, bank deposits are created when they are issued in return for either

______________ or ______________ . As a result, the balance sheet of banks appears as follows (fill in the blanks):

Assets	*Liabilities*
Federal Reserve Notes	____________ ____________
Securities	

10.58
You will recall that earlier it was noted that because total income must equal total expenditure for every borrower who spends more than his income there must be a ______________ who spends *(more/less)* than his income.

Answers

54. securities · Federal Reserve Notes
55. money · is not · money
56. security · bank deposits
57. currency · securities (either order) · bank deposits
58. lender · less

10.59

If securities were the only financial asset that existed, then the assets that these lenders accumulated with their unspent income would be the ______________ that borrowers issue to spend more than their income. That is, if securities were the only type of financial asset, the financial assets of *(creditors/debtors)* would be the financial liabilities of *(creditors/debtors)*.

10.60

Assuming for the moment that securities are the only type of financial asset, suppose that there were $500 billion in outstanding securities. If you were to look at the financial entries in the balance sheets for all debtors and all creditors, all the outstanding securities would appear on the ______________ side for the debtors and on the ______________ side for the creditors, as follows:

Debtors		*Creditors*	
Assets	*Liabilities*	*Assets*	*Liabilities*
	Securities ... $500 billion	Securities ... $500 billion	

10.61

As has been indicated previously, however, securities *(are/are not)* the only type of financial asset that can be accumulated with unspent income. Creditors also have the option of holding their financial assets in the form of ____________.

10.62

Any income not spent for real commodities results in an increase in creditors' holdings of financial assets, whether in the form of money or securities. If nothing is done with the unspent income, it accumulates as ______________. The alternative, of course, is to purchase ______________.

10.63

Also, for any period, because total income and total expenditure must be equal, the amount of income not spent for real commodities by creditors just matches

Answers

59. securities · creditors · debtors
60. liabilities · assets
61. are not · money
62. money · securities

the excess of expenditure over income of debtors. That is, for any period, the increase in *(assets/liabilities)* ___ of creditors must equal the increase in *(assets/liabilities)* ___ of debtors.

10.64
The increase in assets of creditors is, in general, partly _______________ and partly _______________. The increase in liabilities of debtors, however, is composed entirely of _______________.

10.65
As a result, all the outstanding securities must be equal to the holdings of money and securities by creditors. Thus, the amount of securities held by creditors must be *(more/less)* ___ than the total amount of securities outstanding.

10.66
That is, if creditors hold part of their financial assets in the form of money, they *(can/cannot)* ___ hold all the outstanding liabilities, or securities, of debtors. Who then holds the securities that are not held by creditors?

10.67
The answer to this question can be found in the explanation of how money is created. You will recall that money is created when either the Federal Reserve or commercial banks buy _______________. Thus, for every dollar of money held by creditors, the Federal Reserve and the commercial banks hold a dollar of _______________. That is, the securities not held by creditors are held by the _______________ _______________ and _______________ _______________.

10.68
The Federal Reserve and the commercial banks, then, act as *financial intermediaries* between creditors and debtors. The part of creditors' assets held as money appears as liabilities for the financial _______________. These liabilities are

Answers

63. assets · liabilities
64. money · securities · securities
65. less
66. cannot
67. securities · securities · Federal Reserve · commercial banks
68. intermediaries

matched exactly by the securities held by the ____________ ____________ because, in the act of purchasing securities, the financial intermediaries created the money in existence.

10.69

Previously, the financial entries in the balance sheets of creditors and debtors were considered in the case where securities were the only type of financial asset. In that case, all existing securities appeared as *(assets/liabilities)* for creditors and *(assets/liabilities)* for debtors.

10.70

Now, in the more general case with both money and securities as financial assets, suppose that there were $500 billion in outstanding securities and $200 billion in money. If you were to look at the financial entries in the balance sheets of creditors, debtors, and financial intermediaries, you would find that money would appear on the asset side for ____________ and on the liabilities side for ____________ ____________.

10.71

Because money is created when financial intermediaries purchase ____________, there will be $ ____________ billion in securities held as assets by financial intermediaries to balance the money, or liabilities, they have issued.

10.72

Thus, in the general case where there are two types of financial assets (money and securities), part of the existing securities will appear on the assets side of the balance sheet of creditors and the rest on the assets side of ____________ ____________. All the securities will still be on the liabilities side of the balance sheet of ____________.

Answers

68. financial intermediaries
69. assets · liabilities
70. creditors · financial intermediaries
71. securities · 200
72. financial intermediaries · debtors

10.73

In this example, the balance sheets would appear as follows (fill in the missing figures):

Debtors

Assets	*Liabilities*
	Securities . . . $500 billion

Creditors

Assets	*Liabilities*
Securities . . . $____ billion Money (currency and bank deposits) . . . $200 billion	

Financial Intermediaries
(Federal Reserve and Commercial Banks)

Assets	*Liabilities*
Securities . . . $____ billion	Money (currency and bank deposits) . . . $____ billion

10.74

Thus, creditors lend to debtors directly when they acquire the ____________ issued by debtors. In effect, creditors can also lend indirectly by accumulating the liabilities of ____________ ____________, which in turn make loans to debtors.

10.75

Money is created whenever financial intermediaries purchase securities and pay for them with their liabilities. The two kinds of money, currency and bank deposits, are the liabilities of the ____________ ____________ and ____________ ____________. These institutions are called financial intermediaries because they hold ____________ (the liabilities of debtors) while creditors hold ____________ (the liabilities of financial intermediaries.)

Answers

73. 300 · 200 · 200
74. securities · financial intermediaries
75. Federal Reserve · commercial banks (either order) · securities · money

10.76

Creditors, therefore, lend to debtors directly by holding ________________, and indirectly by holding ________________, which enables financial intermediaries to hold securities.

10.77

The more securities financial intermediaries buy, the greater will be the supply of ________________. And, the greater the supply of money, the lower will be the ________________ of ________________.

10.78

Because a purchase of securities by financial intermediaries will *(raise/lower)* the rate of interest, it will lead to *(an increase/a decrease)* in investment expenditure and, consequently, an increase in ________________ ________________.

REVIEW QUESTIONS

10.1

Which of the following are rational explanations why a person might hold part of his wealth in the form of money even though money does not yield any interest?

1. To avoid the costs of selling securities each time he wants to purchase a good or service.
2. To avoid the risk of changes in the value of securities due to interest rate changes.
   a. 1 only
   b. 2 only
   c. both 1 and 2
   d. neither 1 nor 2

A person's wealth can be held in different forms. If we imagine the typical wealth owner confronted with the choice of holding money or securities or some com-

Answers

76. securities · money
77. money · rate · interest
78. lower · an increase · aggregate demand

bination of the two, how will he decide to invest his wealth? Will he invest it all in securities to maximize his interest income? If our wealth owner will be making purchases of goods and services from time to time, he might find that the brokerage and time costs involved in converting securities into cash at the time of expenditure would outweigh the interest earned. In that event, he would want to hold some cash for transactions purposes. If our investor disliked uncertainty about the value of his assets, he might like to give up some interest income by holding part of his wealth in the form of cash, the value of which will not fluctuate as interest rates rise and fall. The correct response is c.

10.2

Which of the following explains why a decrease in the quantity of money will result in a rise in the rate of interest?

1. The quantity of money demanded decreases as the rate of interest increases.
2. The demand curve for money slopes downward from left to right.
3. The quantity of securities demanded increases as the rate of interest increases.
   a. 1 only
   b. 2 only
   c. 1 and 2 only
   d. 1, 2, and 3

When interest rates are relatively low, asset holders will want to hold more money and less securities because they have to give up less interest to avoid the risk and selling costs that come with holding securities. All three statements express this idea. Because of this inverse relationship between the quantity of money demanded and the rate of interest, it is only at a higher rate of interest that the excess demand for money (created by the decrease in the supply of money) will be eliminated. The correct response is d.

10.3

If a commercial bank makes a loan, which of the following would be true?

1. The bank acquires a security.
2. The bank issues a liability.
3. The bank increases the money supply.
   a. 1 only
   b. 1 and 3 only
   c. 2 and 3 only
   d. 1, 2, and 3

When the bank makes a loan, it acquires the IOU of the borrower; therefore, 1 is true. When it makes a loan, it opens a bank account in the name of the borrower. That is, it issues a liability, the new deposits it creates; therefore, 2 is true. Because bank deposits are counted as part of the money supply, when a bank issues new deposits, it adds to the money supply; therefore, 3 is true. The correct response is d.

10.4

Which of the following would be the result of a purchase of securities by a financial intermediary?

1. An increase in the money supply.
2. An increase in the rate of interest.
3. An increase in the supply of securities.
   a. 1 only
   b. 1 and 2 only
   c. 2 only
   d. 2 and 3 only

The money supply is composed of currency plus bank deposits; that is, the liabilities of financial intermediaries. When either the Federal Reserve or commercial banks buy securities, they pay for them by issuing liabilities. The effect of this transaction is to increase the money supply and reduce the supply of securities available to the public. When the money supply increases, it has the effect of reducing the rate of interest. The correct response is a.

11

Monetary Policy

11.1
In the preceding two chapters, the connection between the money supply, the interest rate, and aggregate demand was discussed. The money supply is composed of ________________ and bank ________________ , which are the liabilities of the Federal Reserve and commercial banks.

11.2
The money supply changes whenever the Federal Reserve or commercial banks buy or sell ________________ , because they pay or are paid for the securities with ________________ or bank ________________ .

11.3
A change in the money supply will affect the ________________ rate because the amount of money consumers and businesses are willing to hold increases as the interest rate *(increases/decreases)* .

Answers

1. currency · deposits
2. securities · currency · deposits
3. interest · decreases

11.4

Suppose that the money market is in equilibrium, which means that at the existing interest rate the quantities of money supplied and demanded are ________________. Then, for example, if the money supply is increased, at the initial interest rate, the quantity of money demanded is *(greater/less)* than the than the quantity supplied.

11.5

At that interest rate, consumers and businesses would not be satisfied with their situation and would try to eliminate the excess supply of money by buying securities. This would tend to drive *(up/down)* the value of securities and drive *(up/down)* the interest rate, until the quantity of money demanded *(increased/decreased)* enough to match the quantity supplied.

11.6

Changes in the money supply and the resulting changes in the interest rate will have an effect on ________________ expenditure. As the interest rate decreases, for example, more investment projects will be worth undertaking and firms will *(increase/decrease)* investment expenditure.

11.7

The autonomous changes in investment expenditure that result from changes in the interest rate lead to autonomous changes in ________________ demand. These changes in aggregate demand will have a ________________ effect on real GNP.

11.8

You are now in a position to see how the government can influence the rate of interest. As you know, when the Federal Reserve buys securities from the public, in effect, it issues ________________ in order to pay for them. Suppose that the money market is initially in equilibrium. This means that the rate of interest is

Answers

4. equal · less
5. up · down · increased
6. investment · increase
7. aggregate · multiplier
8. money (currency)

at a level where the quantities of money ______________ and ______________ are equal. Suppose now that the Federal Reserve buys more securities. The effect of this action will be to *(increase/decrease)* the supply of money and *(increase/decrease)* the rate of interest.

11.9

Similarly, if the Federal Reserve decided to sell securities in the money market, it would give securities to asset holders in return for outstanding Federal Reserve liabilities, which is ______________ . As a result, the supply of ______________ would decrease, and the supply of ______________ not held by the Federal Reserve would increase. The effect of this change would be to *(increase/decrease)* the rate of interest.

11.10

Thus, through the buying and selling of ______________ in the money market the Federal Reserve can change the rate of interest. Such action is called *open market operations.* If the Federal Reserve wants to raise the rate of interest, it can do so by carrying out ______________ ______________ operations in the form of *(buying/selling)* securities.

11.11

Selling securities to *(increase/decrease)* the supply of money and thereby *(increasing/decreasing)* the rate of interest, is an example of ______________ ______________ ______________ .

11.12

It is sometimes easy to get confused on the effect of open market operations. Remember, a sale of securities by the Federal Reserve to the public *(increases/decreases)* the supply of securities held by the public. As a result, an open market sale by the Federal Reserve drives the rate of interest *(up/down)* . And, an open market purchase drives the rate of interest *(up/down)* .

Answers

8. supplied · demanded (either order) · increase · decrease
9. money (currency) · money · securities · increase
10. securities · open market · selling
11. decrease · increasing · open market operations
12. increases · up · down

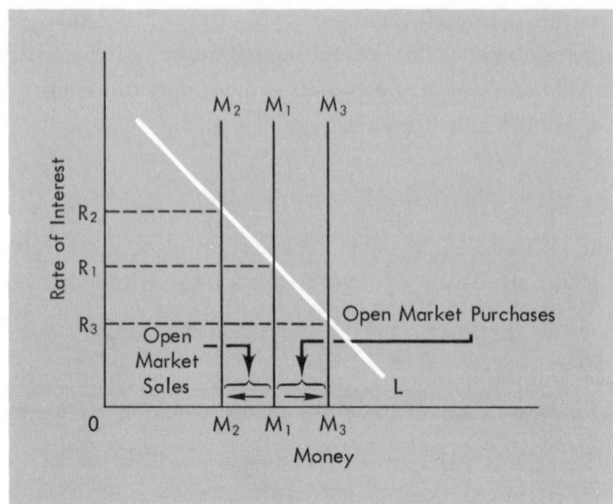

FIGURE 11.1 Open market operations

11.13

This can be seen in a diagram showing the supply and demand for money. In Figure 11.1, L and M_1 are the initial demand and supply curves. The rate of interest determined by these two curves is ________________ .

11.14

If the Federal Reserve makes open market sales of securities, the supply curve of money will shift from M_1 to *(M_2M_3)* . At the initial rate of interest, the market would not be in ________________ , and the rate of interest would rise until it reached a level of ________________ . That is, the market value of securities would be driven *(up/down)* by Federal Reserve open market sales.

11.15

Open market purchases would have the opposite effect. In this case, the money supply would shift from M_1 to ________________ , and the rate of interest would shift from $0R_1$ to ________________ .

Answers

13. $0R_1$
14. M_2 · equilibrium · $0R_2$ · down
15. M_3 · $0R_3$

11.16

Federal Reserve open market sales to and purchases from the public are not the only way in which the money supply and the rate of interest can be changed. Because the Federal Reserve is the government agency that regulates the banking system, it can also take action that encourages commercial banks to purchase or sell securities and thereby increase or decrease the supply of ______________ and raise or lower the ______________ of ______________. (Remember that in this book when a bank makes a loan it is thought of as buying a ______________. Similarly, when a bank decreases its loans, it is thought of as ______________ securities.)

11.17

One of the regulations that commercial banks must follow is the *reserve requirement.* This is a requirement that a certain proportion of their total assets must be held as *reserves* in the form of Federal Reserve Notes or other liabilities of the Federal Reserve. That is, a percentage of banks' total assets must be held as ______________ in the form of Federal Reserve liabilities.

11.18

The main liability of the Federal Reserve, other than Federal Reserve Notes, is commercial bank deposits in the Federal Reserve. Thus, the ______________ requirements can be met by commercial bank holdings of Federal Reserve Notes or commercial bank ______________ in the Federal Reserve.

11.19

Whether a commercial bank holds reserves in the form of Federal Reserve Notes or deposits in the Federal Reserve is a matter of convenience. Either way, it makes no difference to the amount of securities banks can hold because both Federal Reserve liabilities can be used to meet commercial bank ______________ ______________.

Answers

16. money · rate · interest · security · selling
17. reserves
18. reserve · deposits
19. reserve requirements

11.20

If commercial banks had total assets of $200 billion and faced a reserve requirement of 20 percent, their balance sheet might look like this:

Assets		*Liabilities*
Reserves—Federal Reserve Notes and deposits in the Federal Reserve . . .	\$ 40 billion	Bank deposits . . . \$200 billion
Securities . . .	\$160 billion	

If the commercial banks were in this position, they *(could/could not)* ______ buy more securities and create more money because their reserves would then *(fall below/rise above)* ______ the 20 percent reserve requirement.

11.21

Suppose now that the Federal Reserve lowered the reserve requirement to 10 percent. Then the banks would have $40 billion in reserves when they needed only

$ ______ billion. With excess reserves, the banks *(could/could not)* ______ increase their holdings of securities until the excess reserves were eliminated. (Remember again that increasing their holdings of securities often takes the form of *(more/fewer)* ______ loans.)

11.22

With reserves of $40 billion, the banks could increase their total assets until their required reserves were $______ billion. With a reserve requirement of 10 percent, they could increase their total assets to $ ______ billion. Thus, they could increase their holdings of securities by $ ______ and pay for them with new bank deposits of an equal amount.

11.23

It is possible, therefore, for the Federal Reserve to induce commercial banks to increase the money supply by reducing the ______ requirement.

Answers

20. could not · fall below
21. 20 · could · more
22. 40 · 400 · 200
23. reserve

11.24

If the Federal Reserve were to raise the reserve requirement, commercial banks would be forced to *(increase/decrease)* ______ their holdings of securities, which would thereby *(increase/decrease)* ______ the money supply.

11.25

The effect of changing the money supply by a given amount through changes in the reserve requirement will have the same effect as a change in the money supply brought about by open market operations. In both instances, an increase in the money supply will drive the rate of interest *(up/down)* ______ and a decrease will drive the rate of interest *(up/down)* ______ .

11.26

Because commercial banks are required to hold reserves equal to only a fraction of their deposits, the effect of open market operations can be greater than indicated previously. Suppose that the Federal Reserve purchases $10 billion of securities from the public. If $5 billion of the currency created to pay for those securities is deposited in commercial banks, this will *(increase/decrease)* ______ the reserves of commercial banks. If the banks did nothing other than accept the deposit of $5 billion, there would be no further change in the money supply. The public would simply have changed $5 billion of money in the form of ______ into $5 billion in the form of ______ ______ .

11.27

The banks, however, are not likely to do nothing. The deposit of currency will have increased their total assets by $5 billion. All the increase, therefore, comes in the form of *(reserves/securities)* ______ . At the same time, if the reserve requirement is 20 percent of total assets, the increase in the amount of reserves required will be only $ ______ billion.

11.28

Thus, the banks' actual reserves will have increased by $ ______ billion, while the amount required by the Federal Reserve will have increased by

Answers

24. decrease · decrease
25. down · up
26. increase · currency · bank deposits
27. reserves · 1
28. 5

only $ ______________ billion. If the banks initially had no excess reserves, a deposit of $5 billion in currency would leave them with $ ____________ billion in excess reserves.

11.29

With excess reserves, the banks will be able to acquire more ______________ on which they can earn interest. By making more loans to debtors, usually by giving them bank deposits, the commercial banks will acquire new ____________ and at the same time create more ______________ .

11.30

The deposit in commercial banks of part of the money created by Federal Reserve open market purchases from the public makes possible further increases in the money supply because it gives the commercial bank excess ______________ . When banks have excess reserves, they can acquire more ______________ and create more ______________ in the form of bank deposits.

11.31

To repeat an example used earlier, if commercial banks had total assets of $200 billion and faced a reserve requirement of 20 percent, their balance sheet might look like this:

Assets		*Liabilities*
Reserves—Federal Reserve Notes and deposits in the Federal Reserve . . .	$ 40 billion	Bank deposits . . . $ 200 billion
Securities . . .	$160 billion	

In this situation, there would be no excess ______________ , and the banks would be unable to purchase more ______________ .

Answers

28. 1 · 4
29. securities · securities · money
30. reserves · securities · money
31. reserves · securities

11.32

Suppose the Federal Reserve made open market purchases amounting to $10 billion, and $5 billion of the resulting increase in currency was deposited in commercial banks. At first, the banks would find themselves in the following new position:

Assets		*Liabilities*
Reserves–Federal Reserve Notes and deposits in the Federal Reserve . . .	$____billion	Bank deposits . . . $____ billion
Securities . . .	$160 billion	

11.33

In this situation, actual reserves would be $ ______________ billion, but required reserves would be only $ ______________ billion. This means that the banks could expand their holdings of ______________ .

11.34

Banks could buy securities, paying for them with new deposits, until the actual and required ______________ were equal; that is, until there were no ______________ reserves.

11.35

Given their reserves of $45 billion and a reserve requirement of 20 percent, the banks could expand until deposits increased to a level of $ ______________ billion. The final position for the banks would look like this:

Assets		*Liabilities*
Reserves . . .	$ 45 billion	Bank deposits . . . $____billion
Securities . . .	$____billion	

The initial increase in deposits of $5 billion has led the banks to expand deposits by an additional $ ______________ billion so that together deposits increased by $ ______________ billion.

Answers

32. 45 · 205
33. 45 · 41 · securities
34. reserves · excess
35. 225 · 180 · 225 · 20 · 25

11.36

Taking into account the response of the commercial banks, what has been the total effect of the Federal Reserve open market purchases of $10 billion? The money supply has increased by the $5 billion held by consumers and businesses in the form of ______________, plus the increase in bank deposits of $ ______________ billion that resulted when consumers and businesses deposited the other $5 billion of the currency issued by the Federal Reserve.

11.37

The total increase in bank deposits will be a multiple of the amount initially deposited. Space does not permit a full explanation of the banking system multiplier here. But you can see that, with a reserve requirement of 20 percent, an increase in reserves of $1 will permit an increase in total assets of $ ______________. Of this total increase in assets, $ ______________ will be the increase in securities.

11.38

Thus, open market purchases by the Federal Reserve will lead to an increase in the money supply that is *(greater/smaller)* than the increase in currency. The extra money will be created when some of the new currency is deposited in commercial banks, providing the banks with excess ______________, and making it possible for them to buy more ______________. When the commercial banks buy more securities, they will create new bank deposits, which constitutes a further increase in the supply of ______________.

11.39

The same multiple effect could result if the Federal Reserve purchased securities directly from the banks. For example, an open market purchase of $5 billion would reduce banks' holdings of ______________ and increase banks' holdings of ______________ either in the form of Federal Reserve Notes or commercial bank deposits in the Federal Reserve. This would create ______________ reserves and permit a multiple expansion of bank security holdings and bank deposits.

Answers

36. currency · 25
37. 5 · 4
38. greater · reserves · securities · money
39. securities · reserves · excess

11.40

Another, less-important way in which the Federal Reserve can influence the amount of bank deposits in existence is by lending reserves to the commercial banks. This allows banks to meet their reserve requirement by borrowing

_______________ from the Federal Reserve.

11.41

The price banks must pay for these loans is called the *discount rate.* It is called this because the loans are made in an amount from which the interest is deducted, or *discounted.* By changing the _______________ rate, the Federal Reserve can make it more or less expensive to borrow reserves. An increase in the _______________ rate will encourage banks in debt to the Federal Reserve to reduce this debt. To do so, they must sell _______________ , which reduces the _______________ supply.

11.42

A reduction in the _______________ rate will make it less expensive to borrow reserves. This is likely to result in the *(purchase/sale)* ___ of securities and *(an increase/a decrease)* ___ in bank deposits by banks who are willing to borrow reserves at the lower discount rate.

11.43

Of these three policy actions–open _______________ operations, changes in _______________ requirements, and changes in the _______________ rate–open market operations are by far the most important.

11.44

You are now in a position to trace the effects of monetary policy on the economy as a whole. This can be done in terms of Figure 11.2, which has four diagrams. Suppose the economy to be initially in equilibrium, with a money supply curve of M_1 and a rate of interest _______________ , as shown in (i), and an aggregate demand curve of AD_1 and a real GNP of _______________ , as shown in (iv).

Answers

40. reserves
41. discount · discount · securities · money
42. discount · purchase · an increase
43. market · reserve · discount
44. $0R_1$ · 0Q

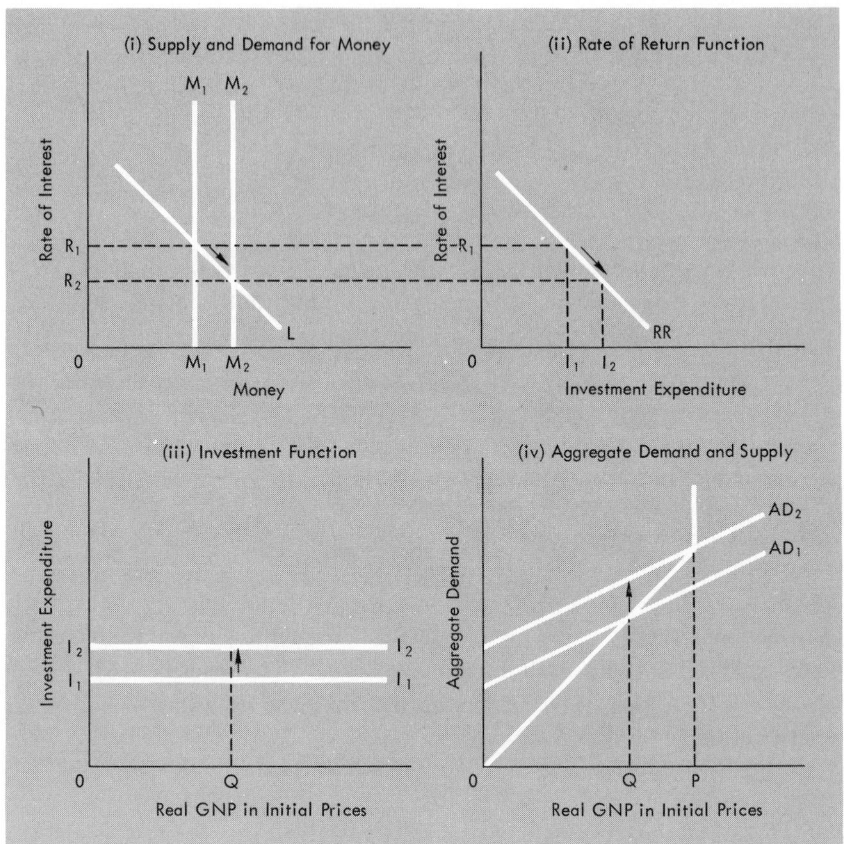

FIGURE 11.2 Monetary policy

11.45

In (ii), the rate of return function RR shows the investment expenditure that would be made at different rates of ________________, given the level of real GNP 0Q. Thus, at the rate of interest $0R_1$, given a real GNP of 0Q, investment expenditure will be ________________.

11.46

In (iii), the investment function shows the investment expenditure (including investment type expenditure made by households) that would be made at

Answers

45. interest · $0I_1$

different levels of ________________ ________________, given the rate of interest $0R_1$. Thus, at a real GNP of 0Q, given the rate of interest $0R_1$, investment expenditure will be ________________. Of course, the amount of $0I_1$ in (ii) and the amount of $0I_1$ in (iii) are equal.

11.47

Suppose now that the government tries to increase aggregate demand by using monetary policy and increases the money supply from OM_1 to OM_2. In (i), this will have the effect of *(increasing/decreasing)* ________ the rate of interest to ________________.

11.48

The decline in the rate of interest will result, as can be seen in (ii), in a movement along the rate of return schedule and *(an increase/a decrease)* ________ in investment expenditure. The level of investment expenditure at the new rate of interest will be ________________.

11.49

The increase in investment expenditure due to a decrease in the rate of interest will appear as a *(shift in/movement along)* ________ the investment function in (iii). At the lower rate of interest, the investment function will be in the *(higher/lower)* ________ position of I_2. At the new rate of interest, with the original level of real GNP 0Q, investment expenditure will be ________________.

11.50

The upward shift of the investment function will have the effect of shifting the aggregate demand curve in (iv) from AD_1 to AD_2. This will have a multiplier effect on real GNP, which will *(increase/decrease)* ________ from 0Q to ________________.

11.51

With the new money supply of OM_2, then, the economy *(will/will not)* ________ have full employment without inflation. In this situation, then, the increase in the

Answers

46. real GNP · $0I_1$
47. decreasing · $0R_2$
48. an increase · $0I_2$
49. shift in · higher · $0I_2$
50. increase · 0P
51. will

money supply from OM_1 to OM_2 *(was/was not)* ________ the appropriate action for the Federal Reserve to have taken.

11.52

Thus, the government has at least two types of policy that can be used to fight unemployment or inflation. It can change taxes or government expenditure to influence aggregate demand, which would be ____________ policy. Or it can take action that leads to a change in the money supply, which would be ____________ policy.

REVIEW QUESTIONS

11.1

Assume the balance sheet of all commercial banks was as follows:

Assets	*Liabilities*
Currency $80 billion	Deposits $320 billion
Securities $240 billion	

If the reserve requirement was 20 percent of deposits, by how much could the commercial banks expand loans and deposits without receiving additional deposits of currency? $ ____________ billion.

a. 80
b. 16
c. 0
d. none of the above

In the initial situation, banks held $80 billion in reserves, but they were required to hold only 20 percent of $320 billion (or $64 billion) in reserves. The banks could expand their holdings of securities, paying for them with new deposits, as long as their actual reserves ($80 billion) exceeded their required reserves (20 percent of deposits). If they added $80 billion to securities by issuing new deposits to their borrowers, total securities would be $320 billion, deposits would be $400 billion, and actual reserves would just equal required reserves. The correct response is a.

Answers

51. was
52. fiscal · monetary

11.2

An economy is at full employment, and the price level is relatively stable. Many people, however, have protested that the government's policy of promoting rapid economic growth places too much emphasis on future consumption and too little on present consumption.

Which of the following could satisfy the protestors' wishes without causing more inflation or more unemployment?

1. A reduction in income taxes.
2. An increase in interest rates.
3. An increase in government expenditure.
   a. 1 taken by itself
   b. 2 taken by itself
   c. 1 and 2 taken together
   d. 1 and 3 taken together

At full employment, an increase in consumption expenditure would be possible only if there were a corresponding decrease in real government and/or investment expenditure. Thus, if consumers wish to increase present consumption at the expense of future consumption, resources will have to be directed from the production of investment goods to the production of consumption goods. The reduced investment would make future consumption lower than it otherwise would be but would make possible higher present consumption. Of the policies given, a reduction in income taxes would generate an increase in consumption expenditure, and an increase in interest rates would be appropriate to reduce investment expenditure. Both responses a and d would be inflationary, and response b would lead to higher unemployment. The correct response is c.

11.3

"The more money there is in the economy, the more people spend. The more people spend, the higher the national income. Therefore, the greater the supply of money, the better off people are."

Which of the following is true?

a. The statement is incorrect because more money in the economy does not usually lead to more spending.
b. The statement is correct because an increase in spending can lead to an increase in income.
c. The statement is incorrect because real income is limited by the economy's capacity to produce.
d. The statement is correct because the amount of money in the economy determines how well off people are.

Although it is true, given unemployed resources, that an increase in the money supply can stimulate aggregate demand and thus increase real national output and living standards, it does not follow that people always will be better off, the greater the money supply. Classic cases of too much money causing rampant inflation and economic collapse are not unknown. Thus, although an increase in the money supply is one of the weapons of monetary policy used to stimulate the economy in a recession, the upper limit to the real output of a nation is determined by the nation's productive resources. The correct response is c.

11.4

Which of the following types of people would suffer a loss in wealth from an unexpected rise in the rate of interest?

1. Persons whose assets consist entirely of money.
2. Persons whose assets consist entirely of securities.
   a. 1 only
   b. 2 only
   c. both 1 and 2
   d. neither 1 nor 2

If the going rate of interest were 6 percent, you would be able to buy a security that promised to pay $106 at the end of one year for $100. Conversely, in a perfect market, you would be able to sell such a security for $100. If, however, after you had purchased this security for $100, the rate of interest were to rise to 8 percent, you would no longer be able to sell your security for $100. At the price of $100, this security will only return 6 percent and anyone with $100 can buy a security that will now pay $108 at the end of the year. You would be able to sell this security for approximately $98.15 because only at this lower price would a promise to pay $106 in one year yield a rate of return of 8 percent. Persons holding securities, therefore, suffer a capital loss when interest rates unexpectedly rise because the value of securities and interest rates are inversely related. Only persons holding money will not suffer a loss through an unexpected interest rate rise. The correct response is b.

12

Problems of a Dynamic Economy

12.1
In Chapters 5 through 7, a simple model was used to explain how ____________ ________________ determines whether there will be unemployment, inflation, or full employment without inflation. In Chapters 8 through 11, you learned how the government can influence aggregate demand through ________________ and ________________ policy to help avoid unemployment or inflation.

12.2
The ideas developed in these chapters are basically simple ideas. Given the widely accepted goals of full employment and average price stability, your reaction may very well be that it should be simple to avoid unemployment and inflation by applying these ideas to actual policy. But, as you know, the Amercian economy *(has/has not)* had periods of unemployment and of inflation.

Answers

1. aggregate demand · fiscal · monetary
2. has

12.3

This record does not necessarily indicate, however, that the theories presented in the preceding chapters are incorrect. In fact, many economists argue that much of the unemployment and inflation of the past resulted because the government did not use the policies suggested by these theories. These economists feel that had their theories been followed, much of this unemployment and inflation *(would/would not)* ______ have been avoided.

12.4

There has, however, been a growing acceptance of the basic ideas presented in this book among government policy makers. For example, after a period of high unemployment from 1958–1963, the government followed these ideas and decreased taxes in order to reduce unemployment. The subsequent reduction of the unemployment rate from 5.5 percent in 1963 to 4.0 percent by the end of 1965 suggests that the kind of fiscal policy suggested by economic theory *(will/will not)* ______ work.

12.5

But, even if there were complete acceptance of these ideas, several factors that were excluded from the simplified discussion of the preceding chapters may make it difficult to make the correct policy decisions. That is, the real world is *(more/less)* ______ complicated than it appears in the models analyzed in Chapters 5–11, and real-life complications can make it *(more/less)* ______ difficult to choose the right policies than seems apparent at first.

12.6

One complication that policy makers must take into account is the continuous growth of the Amercian economy. Most of the previous analysis was concerned with how policy is aimed at equating aggregate demand and a given ______ ______ in initial prices. But, because population increase results in growth of the labor force, because investment expenditure results in growth of the stock of capital goods, and because technological change results in increased productivity of the economy's resources, potential GNP *(remains/does not remain)* ______ constant.

Answers

3. would
4. will
5. more · more
6. potential GNP · does not remain

12.7

Because continuous growth in the quantity and productivity of resources means continuous growth of potential GNP, in order to achieve full employment without inflation it is necessary to have continuous growth of ________________ ________________.

12.8

This means, of course, that the level of aggregate demand that was adequate in achieving those goals last year will be too *(great/small)* this year. Therefore, unless policy makers take into account the growth in potential GNP, policy that was successful last year will result in *(inflation/unemployment)* this year.

12.9

Keeping track of the growth in potential GNP is not the only difficulty that arises from the dynamic, changing nature of the economy. Nor is it the most serious difficulty. Because the growth in the quantity and productivity of resources takes place at a fairly steady rate, it *(is/is not)* possible to get a relatively accurate forecast of future growth in potential GNP from what has happened to potential GNP in the recent past. Unfortunately, this is not always true of other variables that are of importance to policy makers.

12.10

If the goal is to have full employment without inflation, you know from the simple model that it is necessary to have growth in aggregate demand, matching the growth in potential GNP. But what changes this will require in the policy variables–such as taxes, government expenditure, or the money supply–depend on what autonomous changes there will be in consumption and investment expenditure independent of government action. That is, if other factors will cause a change in aggregate demand, the government *(must/need not)* know what they will be before it can properly decide what actions to undertake. In other words, to make the right policy decisions the government must be able to *forecast* *(only/not only)* how its actions will change aggregate demand, but *(not/also)* how other factors will change aggregate demand.

Answers

7. aggregate demand
8. small · unemployment
9. is
10. must · not only · also

12.11

For example, suppose that this year aggregate demand was at just the right level to achieve full employment without inflation. Suppose also that the government accurately forecasts a growth in potential GNP of 4 percent between this year and next. Economic theory tells you that to keep the economy at full employment without inflation aggregate demand must grow by ______________ percent between this year and next. If it grows more than that, the result would be ______________. If it grows less than that, the result would be __________.

12.12

In this situation, it matters *(little/a great deal)* how much private expenditure will change as a result of factors other than government policy. It also is of considerable importance how accurately the government can ______________ this change.

12.13

For example, suppose consumers and businesses expected many commodities to become scarce and increased their expenditure enough to raise aggregate demand by 5 percent in the absence of any change in government policy. If this were the case, the correct policy would be to use fiscal and monetary policy to *(increase/decrease)* aggregate demand by ______________ percent from what it would otherwise be.

12.14

In this example, if the government was unable to forecast accurately the autonomous increase in private expenditure and used fiscal and monetary policy to increase aggregate demand by 4 percent in addition to the unforseen autonomous increase in demand, the result would be ______________. A situation similar to this occurred in 1951 when consumers and businesses reacted to the start of the Korean War by stockpiling many commodities. This unanticipated increase in aggregate demand resulted in a 7 percent increase in the price level (GNP deflator).

Answers

11. 4 · inflation · unemployment
12. a great deal · forecast
13. decrease · 1
14. inflation

12.15

To take another example, discoveries of new products lead businesses to acquire the capital goods necessary to produce them. Suppose that this year fewer discoveries than normal are made. With a given rate of interest, businesses *(would/would not)* find as many profitable investment opportunities as in the past and, other things equal, investment expenditure would *(increase/decrease)* .

12.16

Suppose the decrease in investment expenditure were enough, in the absence of other changes, to cause an autonomous decrease in aggregate demand of 6 percent. Again supposing potential GNP were to increase by 4 percent this year, fiscal and monetary policy should be used to add to aggregate demand an autonomous increase of ______________ percent: ______________ percent to offset the decline in investment expenditure and ______________ percent to match the growth in potential GNP.

12.17

If the decline in investment expenditure were not forecast by the government, and fiscal and monetary policy were used to increase aggregate demand by only enough to match the growth in potential GNP, the result would be __________.

12.18

Most of the recessions, as well as the Great Depression, have resulted primarily from a decline in investment expenditure that was not sufficiently offset by increases in other types of expenditure to keep aggregate demand from falling below potential GNP in initial prices. This means, of course, that the appropriate fiscal and monetary policies *(were/were not)* used. One explanation is that until recently these modern theories were not generally recognized, and at other times the government *(was/was not)* willing to use the policies suggested by modern economic theory. But, even if the government had always been willing to adopt rational policies, in order to decide on the right course of action it would still have been necessary to ______________ correctly the changes in investment expenditure brought about by other factors.

Answers

15. would not · decrease
16. 10 · 6 · 4
17. unemployment
18. were not · was not · forecast

12.19

Thus, it may be difficult to choose the right policy because it may be difficult to ______________ accurately what changes in aggregate demand will occur because of changes in expectations, in the rate of discovery of new products, and other such factors.

12.20

Because it may often be impossible to forecast changes in aggregate demand due to other factors, the government may find out about the change only after unemployment or inflation has occurred. In this situation, fiscal and monetary policy *(can/cannot)* ______ be used to prevent the problem, but they *(can/cannot)* ______ be used to alleviate it.

12.21

You have seen that fiscal and monetary policy must continuously be adjusted to avoid unemployment or inflation. Fiscal and monetary policy must be adjusted not only to keep aggregate demand growing along with ______________ ______________, but to offset changes in ______________ ______________ due to other factors.

12.22

In order to choose the "right" policy, it is necessary to ______________ correctly both changes in potential GNP and changes in aggregate demand due to other factors. Changes in potential GNP are relatively *(easy/difficult)* ______ to forecast accurately, because the quantity and productivity of resources grow at a relatively steady rate. Changes in aggregate demand due to other factors, however, do not occur in a regular fashion and are relatively *(easy/difficult)* ______ to forecast accurately.

12.23

When the government does not forecast changes in aggregate demand correctly, it *(will/will not)* ______ be able to determine what is the right policy in time to avoid inflation or unemployment.

Answers

19. forecast
20. cannot · can
21. potential GNP · aggregate demand
22. forecast · easy · difficult
23. will not

12.24

In addition to the time lag involved in identifying the nature and size of the problem, a considerable length of time may be required by Congress or other government policy makers to decide exactly what policies should be undertaken and to put the policies into effect. Suppose the government were to be caught by surprise by a rise in the unemployment rate from 4 percent to 7 percent in just a few months. Before a tax cut, for example, could be put into effect, the President must make a proposal to Congress, there must be hearings on the proposal, and a bill must be written and enacted into law. Because all this takes

________________ to be done, an immediate application of economic theory to fiscal policy is practically *(possible/impossible)* even when the exact nature of the problem is known.

12.25

The example of the large tax cut of 1964 gives an indication of the time it can take for the government to act. The decision to propose a tax cut was made by President Kennedy in the summer of 1962, but it took until February 1964 for the tax cut to be passed and to go into effect. The cost of the delay was that the unemployment rate remained *(higher/lower)* for a *(longer/shorter)* period of time than would otherwise have been the case.

12.26

A more recent example is the 10 percent tax increase that President Johnson proposed in 1966, when inflation threatened, that was not passed until 1968 when inflation was already underway. The purpose of the tax increase was to

(increase/decrease) aggregate demand to stop ________________. Because of the delay in being enacted, it was too late to prevent inflation.

12.27

Because of the delays that necessarily result from the nature of the political process, many economists have urged that arrangements be made to put specific policies into effect automatically once the problem is recognized. Such an arrangement would have the advantage of helping eliminate unemployment or inflation *(more/less)* quickly.

Answers

24. time · impossible
25. higher · longer
26. decrease · inflation
27. more

12.28

Actually, there are some policies that are automatically put into effect when employment or inflation occurs. For example, when unemployment increases, the payment of unemployment compensation to workers without jobs *(increases/decreases)* ______. Unemployment compensation is an example of a *(government expenditure/transfer payment)* ______ that increases automatically when unemployment increases.

12.29

As with any other transfer payment, an increase in unemployment compensation results in *(an increase/a decrease)* ______ in aggregate demand. As a result, the decline in aggregate demand, relative to potential GNP in initial prices, that caused unemployment would be *(deepened/offset)* ______ to some extent by the unemployment compensation program.

12.30

Arrangements that put policies into effect automatically are called *built-in stabilizers.* The unemployment compensation program is an example of a

______ ______ because when unemployment increases it automatically increases *(government expenditure/transfer payments)* ______.

12.31

Another example of a built-in stabilizer is the federal income tax structure. Because the amount of income taxes collected by the government depends on the size of the national income, whenever income increases income tax receipts *(increase/decrease)* ______. As a result, when there is inflation, income in current prices increases and tax receipts *(increase/decrease)* ______. When there is a recession and income falls, tax receipts *(increase/decrease)* ______.

12.32

In each case, given the goal of full employment with no inflation, the changes in tax receipts that result automatically when inflation or recession occurs are in the *(right/wrong)* ______ direction. That is, the tax structure tends to stabilize the econ-

Answers

28. increases · transfer payment
29. an increase · offset
30. built-in stabilizer · transfer payments
31. increase · increase · decrease
32. right

omy because it results in tax *(increases/decreases)* when there is inflation and tax *(increases/decreases)* when there is unemployment.

12.33

Both the unemployment compensation program and the tax structure are examples of ______ ______ because they automatically change transfer payments and tax receipts in the right direction when the economy deviates from full employment without inflation. Unfortunately, however, the built-in stabilizers are not sufficient to prevent unemployment or inflation from occurring, but serve only as a partial offset to the changes in ______ ______ that cause the problem.

12.34

Thus, despite the existence of built-in stabilizers, government policies are required to help achieve the goals of full employment and ______ stability. Two time lags posing problems for policy makers are: (a) the time lag involved in identifying the problem, and (b) the time taken to put the appropriate policy into operation. Many economists have urged that an arrangement be made by which it would be possible, immediately upon identification of a problem, to generate the appropriate fiscal stimulus or restraint. The purpose of this arrangement would be to avoid the time lag connected with *(identification of the problem/the decision-making process)*.

12.35

Still a third difficulty exists for policy makers. Once a policy is undertaken, it takes time for it to affect aggregate demand, income, and employment. That is, the full response of aggregate demand to a particular fiscal or monetary policy change ordinarily *(will/will not)* take place immediately.

12.36

For example, an increase in the money supply may reduce the rate of interest, but this may not lead to *(an increase/a decrease)* in investment expenditure until a substantial period of time has elapsed.

Answers

32. increases · decreases
33. built-in stabilizers · aggregate demand
34. price · the decision-making process
35. will not
36. an increase

12.37

To take another example, a decrease in income taxes will increase disposable income, but it may take a considerable length of time before the full *(increase/decrease)* ______ in consumption expenditure will be made by consumers. Consumers take ______ to readjust their spending levels, and the multiplier process takes time to work itself out.

12.38

The uncertain time lag between undertaking a policy and its full effect on aggregate demand makes it *(more/less)* ______ difficult for policy makers to time their actions properly. This lag makes it necessary for the government to forecast changes in the economy *(further/less far)* ______ ahead than would otherwise be the case.

12.39

In summary, you have seen how three types of ______ lags make it difficult to apply the basic ideas analyzed in preceding chapters. These lags stem from the ______ required (a) to identify the problem; (b) to decide what action to take; and (c) for any policy action to have its full effect.

12.40

The difficulties involved in putting theory into practice to eliminate unemployment or inflation are not limited to time lags involved with fiscal and monetary policy. You will recall that in the preceding chapters it was assumed that as long as there was an output gap the price level *(would/would not)* ______ rise. Or, put the other way around, it was assumed that the price level would rise only when there was an ______ gap.

12.41

In the real world, this is not strictly true. If you examine Figures 12.1 and 12.2, you will observe that there have been periods when the unemployment rate was above 4 percent and the rate of inflation was greater than 2 percent. That is, in the real world both unemployment and inflation *(can/cannot)* ______ exist at the same time.

Answers

37. increase · time
38. more · further
39. time · time
40. would not · inflationary
41. can

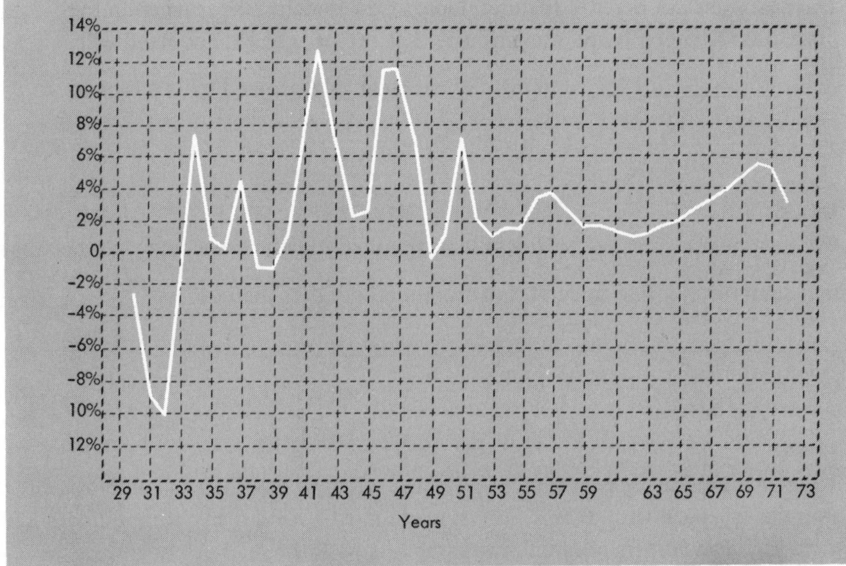

FIGURE 12.1 Change in GNP deflator, 1930–1972

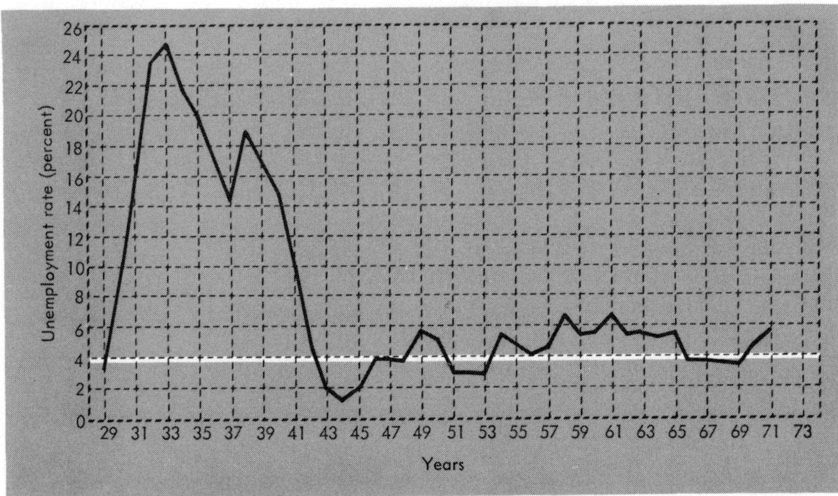

FIGURE 12.2 Unemployment rate, 1929–1972

12.42

This fact does not destroy the usefulness of the conclusions reached in the preceding chapters. It still remains true that excess aggregate demand will cause ________________ and insufficient aggregate demand will cause ________________.

12.43

What was assumed away for the sake of simplicity in the preceding chapters was that sometimes inflation can result from factors other than excess ________________ ________________. Thus, in fact, there *(can/cannot)* be both inflation and unemployment at the same time.

12.44

To understand one reason that inflation can occur at less than full employment, consider a typical firm. If this firm is in an industry with many competitors, the price it charges for its product must be in line with the market price. Otherwise, it *(would/would not)* be very difficult to sell much of its output. But if the firm is in a market with only a few competitors and it produces a product that is not exactly the same as any of its competitors', the firm will have considerably *(more/less)* independence when setting its price.

12.45

In the United States, many markets are characterized by only limited competition, with the result that many firms have *(considerable/practically no)* leeway in setting their prices.

12.46

Although it is very difficult to prove, many economists believe that firms in markets with limited competition customarily set their prices to cover costs plus a percentage margin of profit. For example, if costs are 80 cents per unit and a firm charges $1 per unit, it is setting its price to cover ________________ plus a profit margin equal to ________________ percent of the price.

Answers

42. inflation · unemployment
43. aggregate demand · can
44. would · more
45. considerable
46. costs · 20

12.47

If firms actually do set prices this way, whenever there is a rise in costs per unit of output there will also be a rise in ______________ . Thus, a factor that can cause inflation, even when there is unemployment, is a *(rise/fall)* in ______________ per unit of output.

12.48

Why might unit costs rise during a period of unemployment? One situation in which unit costs might rise is when firms are expanding their rate of production very rapidly. That is, a firm may be able to expand its rate of production without a rise in unit costs if the expansion is spread out over a *(long/short)* period of time. But if it tries to expand its rate of production quickly, its unit costs are likely to *(rise/fall)* .

12.49

A rapid increase in the rate of production may lead to *(increasing/decreasing)* unit costs because firms may have to pay higher prices for materials to get them delivered promptly. Or it may not be able to find the best combination of labor skills immediately and must settle for second best. If firms set prices to cover costs plus a ______________ margin, the increase in unit costs will lead to ______________ increases.

12.50

Thus, if the economy is moving toward full employment very rapidly, many firms in the economy will be increasing their rate of production *(rapidly/gradually)* . As a result, many firms will incur *(higher/lower)* unit costs and will *(raise/lower)* prices to preserve their desired profit margins.

12.51

Look back to Figures 12.1 and 12.2, which show changes in the price level and the unemployment rate. In 1934, for example, even though the unemployment rate was very *(high/low)* it fell sharply, and real GNP rose by 9 percent. At the same time, there was a fairly *(high/low)* rate of inflation, almost 8 percent.

Answers

47. prices · rise · costs
48. long · rise
49. increasing · profit · price
50. rapidly · highly · raise
51. high · high

12.52

Another reason that costs might rise when there is unemployment is that wages for many workers are not determined in highly competitive markets. As a result, it is possible for wages to rise even though there is an excess supply of labor. For example, suppose that there is an unemployment rate of 6 percent. If the labor market were highly competitive, you would expect wage rates to *(rise/fall)* . But, many wage rates are determined in collective bargaining between unions and employers, and unions may push wage rates up even though there is unemployment.

12.53

An increase in wage rates does not by itself necessarily raise unit costs, however. Technical change, which tends to increase the productivity of workers each year, must also be taken into account. For example, if labor productivity were to increase by 3 percent between this year and next, it would mean that the same amount of output could be produced next year with 3 percent *(more/fewer)* workers. If wages were to remain constant between this year and next, the labor cost per unit of output would *(rise/fall/remain the same)* .

12.54

This can be seen in Table 12.1. In this example, next year it will require *(more/fewer)* men to produce 1,000 units of output because labor ________ will have increased.

12.55

An increase in labor productivity from 10.0 to 10.3 units of output per man will reduce the labor required to produce 1,000 units from ________ to ________ men. As a result, if the annual wage paid to a man is $1,000 in each year, the total labor cost will fall from $ ________ to $ ________ .

Answers

52. fall
53. fewer · fall
54. fewer · productivity
55. 100 · 97 · 100,000 · 97,000

Table 12.1

LABOR PRODUCTIVITY INCREASES AND UNIT LABOR COSTS

	This year	*Next year*
Output	1,000	1,000
Labor productivity (output per man)	10.0	10.3
Labor requirements (men)	100	97
Wage rate (dollars per man)	$1,000	$1,000
Total labor costs	$100,000	$97,000
Labor costs/unit of output	$______	$______

12.56

It is possible now to calculate unit labor costs in each year. This year, total labor costs were $100,000, and next year they will be $97,000. With output equal to 1,000 in both years, the labor cost per unit of output will decline from

$ __________ to $ __________, which is a drop of __________ percent. (You can enter these unit costs in the table.)

12.57

Thus, if labor productivity rises and wage rates remain unchanged, unit labor costs will *(rise/fall)*. Put another way, if labor productivity rises, it *(will/will not)* be possible to raise wages without increasing unit labor costs.

12.58

In fact, as long as wage rate increases do not exceed labor productivity increases, unit labor costs *(will/will not)* rise. If the wage rate increase exceeds the productivity increase, however, __________ labor costs will *(rise/fall)*.

12.59

In the example given above, because labor __________ rose by 3 percent, it would have been possible to increase the wage rate by __________ percent without raising __________ __________ costs.

Answers

56. 100 · 97 · 3
57. fall · will
58. will not · unit · rise
59. productivity · 3 · unit labor

12.60

A wage rate increase will result in higher unit labor costs only if they exceed the increases in ________________ ________________. If wage rates increased by 4 percent when labor productivity increased by only 3 percent, those firms that set prices to cover costs plus a required profit margin will raise their __________.

12.61

Thus, even if there is no excess aggregate demand, if collective bargaining results in wage rate increases that are greater than labor ________________ increases, the result is likely to be a *(rise/fall)* in the price level. The 1970–1971 period provides a case in point. During this period, the rate of productivity increase was well below average, about 1½ percent per year, while the rate of increase in wages was about 6 percent per year. This implied an increase in unit labor costs of ________________ percent per year.

12.62

If wage rate increases just match labor productivity increases, inflation can result if firms try to increase their profit margins by raising prices. As indicated previously, because many firms operate in markets in which they have few competitors, they *(do/do not)* have considerable control over prices that prevail in those markets. Therefore, it is sometimes possible for these firms to change their profit margins by changing their ________________.

12.63

Thus, it is possible for inflation to result, even if there is no excess aggregate demand, because the markets for many types of labor and for many products *(are/are not)* highly competitive. If unions manage to obtain wage increases in excess of labor ________________ increases, the result can be ________________. Or if firms try to use their control over market prices to increase their ________________ margins, the result can be ________________. In addition, earlier you learned that when output is increasing rapidly, it may result in rising ________________ costs, and the result can be ________________.

Answers

60. labor productivity · prices
61. productivity · rise · 4½
62. do · prices
63. are not · productivity · inflation · profit · inflation · unit · inflation

12.64

Inflation that results from these factors is often called *cost-push inflation.* This term is used to distinguish it from inflation that is due to excess aggregate demand, which is called *demand-pull inflation.* The difference between these two is that ______________ inflation is caused by too great a level of expenditure, and ______________ inflation is caused by rising costs of production.

12.65

Although it is possible for cost-push inflation to occur at any time, it is more likely to occur when the economy is at or near full employment, when the strong market positions of firms and unions tempt them to make inflationary adjustments in profits and wages. Thus, when the economy approaches full employment, ______________ inflation is likely to occur even if there is no excess aggregate demand.

12.66

One situation in which costs are likely to rise even if there is unemployment is when people expect inflation to occur in the future. Suppose, for example, that labor and management in an industry are bargaining over a three-year wage contract. If workers expect prices to rise over the period of the contract, they would require a *(higher/lower)* wage settlement to achieve a given real income increase than if they expected no price change. As a result, negotiated wage increases are likely to be larger when prices are expected to *(rise/fall)*.

12.67

Because people are likely to expect inflation when they have recently experienced it, cost-push inflation frequently follows a period of demand-pull inflation. That is, if in one period prices rose, people are likely to expect prices to *(continue to rise/stop rising)*. The expectation of future inflation will lead workers and other income earners to demand *(higher/lower)* compensation than they would otherwise, thereby raising costs and, ultimately, prices.

Answers

64. demand-pull · cost-push
65. cost-push
66. higher · rise
67. continue to rise · higher

12.68

Thus, a demand-pull inflation, by affecting people's expectations, causes ________________ inflation to occur in subsequent periods. The Nixon Administration believed that this was a major factor in the inflation of 1969–1973. During the 1966–1968 period, the substantial growth in aggregate demand due to the Vietnam military build-up reduced unemployment below 4 percent unemployment and drove the rate of inflation to over 4 percent per year. This was clearly a case of ________________ inflation.

12.69

During the period 1969–1973, unemployment rose well above the 4 percent mark. Despite the elimination of the *(output/inflationary)* gap, however, the rate of inflation remained above 4 percent. Government economists believed that the inflation due to excess aggregate demand in the 1966–1968 period led people to expect continued *(inflation/unemployment)*, and that this in turn led to abnormally *(high/low)* demands for wage increases, with resulting higher costs and prices. This would clearly be a case of *(demand-pull/cost-push)* inflation. A major argument for imposing wage and price controls in 1971 and in 1973 was to eliminate these inflationary expectations.

12.70

Another reason it may be difficult to achieve both full employment and average price stability at the same time is that not all markets will have the same supply and demand conditions. For example, suppose that the government through its fiscal and monetary policy adjusts aggregate demand to just the right level, as suggested by the analysis in terms of the simple model of the preceding chapters. This means that ________________ ________________ is just equal to ________________ ________________ in initial prices. If this model were an exact duplicate of the real world, the economy *(would/would not)* experience both full employment and average price stability.

12.71

In the real world, however, there are many commodities and many markets. Even if aggregate demand were at the "right" level in terms of this model, it

Answers

68. cost-push · demand-pull
69. inflationary · inflation · high · cost-push
70. aggregate demand · potential GNP · would

would generally not be true that at initial prices the amounts demanded and supplied would be equal in all markets. In some markets, at initial prices there would be excess demand, and prices would tend to *(rise/fall)*____ . In other markets, at initial prices there would be excess supply, and, therefore, *(upward/downward)*____ pressure on prices.

12.72

If all markets functioned perfectly, it would be expected that prices in all markets *(would/would not)*____ adjust—some upward and some downward—to their new equilibrium levels. The upward and downward movements in individual prices would cancel each other out, *(leaving/causing)*____ the average price level *(unchanged/to rise)*____ .

12.73

But as you will recall, many markets do not function perfectly. As a result, many individual prices tend to be *(flexible/rigid)*____ in a downward direction.

Thus, in many of the markets that have excess supply prices will not ________ as might be expected.

12.74

At the same time, even in imperfect markets, prices do tend to ________ in response to excess demand. Thus, in a situation in which some markets have excess supply and others excess demand, the expected price *(increases/decreases)*____ would be forthcoming, but the expected price *(increases/decreases)*____ would not be.

12.75

When aggregate demand is at the "right" level, some markets will be characterized by excess supply and others by excess demand at initial prices. Because not all markets function perfectly in this situation, the price increases in the markets with excess demand *(will/will not)*____ be offset by decreases in markets with excess supply, and consequently, the average price level will ________ .

Answers

71. rise · downward
72. would · leaving · unchanged
73. rigid · fall
74. rise · increases · decreases
75. will not · rise

12.76

Thus, even with the theoretically correct level of aggregate demand, because of market imperfections there can be *(no/some)* ______ inflation. In those markets where prices do not fall in response to excess supply, firms will *(increase/decrease)* ______ output and employment. This will occur because when demand falls consumers are not willing to purchase all the commodities that suppliers are willing to produce. Thus, not only will there be some inflation in this situation but there will also be some ______.

12.77

When the economy is far from full employment, there will be few, if any, markets where there is excess *(supply/demand)* ______, and many markets where there is excess ______. In that situation, the average price level *(will/will not)* ______ rise rapidly.

12.78

The closer the economy is to full employment, the more markets there will be that are characterized by excess *(supply/demand)* ______. Consequently, the closer the economy is to full employment, the *(more/fewer)* ______ markets there will be in which prices will rise. That is, the lower the unemployment rate, the higher the rate of ______.

12.79

Earlier, you learned that the closer to full employment, the more costs and prices are likely to rise in markets where there is *(perfect/imperfect)* ______ competition. Now you have learned that because prices rise in markets where there is excess demand, *(and also/but do not)* ______ fall in markets where there is excess ______, the closer the economy is to full employment, the higher the rate of ______. This can be true even when there is no excess aggregate demand.

Answers

76. some · decrease · unemployment
77. demand · supply · will not
78. demand · more · inflation
79. imperfect · but do not · supply · inflation

12.80

This phenomenon of the rate of inflation increasing even when there is no excess aggregate demand is represented in Figure 12.3. The rate of ______________ is measured along the vertical axis, and the rate of ______________ along the horizontal axis. The curve that slopes downward from left to right shows that at low rates of unemployment the rate of inflation tends to be *(high/low)* .

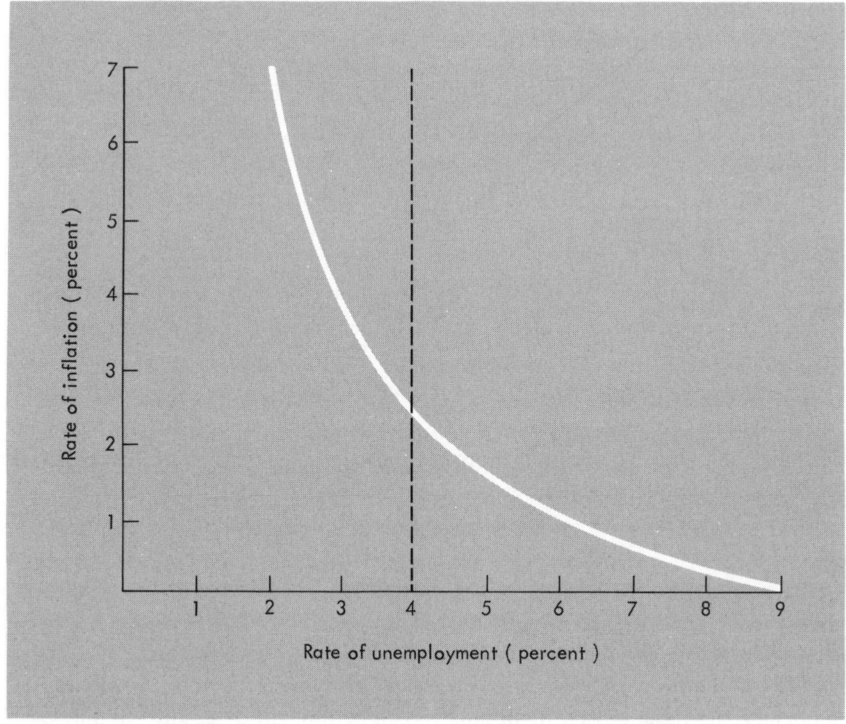

FIGURE 12.3 Example of trade-off between unemployment and inflation

12.81

This curve shows the trade-off between unemployment and inflation from which government policy makers must choose when deciding monetary and fiscal policy. Should they, for example, stimulate aggregate demand so as to maintain low unemployment and thereby accept a relatively *(high/low)* rate of inflation, or should they restrain aggregate demand in order to avoid inflation and thereby accept a relatively *(high/low)* rate of unemployment?

Answers

80. inflation · unemployment · high
81. high · high

12.82

The existence of a trade-off between unemployment and inflation poses a dilemma for policy makers. It makes it difficult to use fiscal and monetary policy to avoid both inflation and unemployment at the same time. If fiscal and monetary policy are used to keep the economy at full employment, some ______________ is likely to occur. If they are used to keep aggregate demand so low that no inflation will occur, then some ______________ will result.

12.83

Faced with this dilemma, the government must choose between two evils. It must decide where along the inflation-unemployment trade-off curve it should aim for. That is, it must decide whether it is worse to be near full employment with some ______________ or to have price stability with some ___________ .

12.84

The decision as to what point policy makers should aim for cannot be decided on the basis of economic analysis alone. The people who are hurt most by inflation and the people who are hurt most by unemployment *(are/are not)* in general the same people. Any decision about which policy to choose will involve dividing the costs of inflation and unemployment among different people in some way. Such a decision is more *(economic/political)* than *(economic/political)* in nature. Consequently, there is no objective or scientific right or wrong decision. Which decision you would support would depend on your point of view.

12.85

In an attempt to avoid facing the dilemma of choosing between evils, economists and political leaders have advocated a variety of policy actions to accompany monetary and fiscal policy. Such policies can be thought of as shifting the trade-off in Figure 12.3 to the *(left/right)* . One action would be wage and price controls. Another would be voluntary wage-price and price restraint according to the wage-price guideposts.

12.86

A longer-run solution that has been advocated by some and regarded as impractical by others is the attempt to make markets more efficient and more

Answers

82. inflation · unemployment
83. inflation · unemployment
84. are not · political · economic
85. left

competitive through antitrust and other government policies, such as improved retraining facilities, employment exchanges, and job information. Whether or not they would work, such proposals are designed to make labor more mobile and prices more responsive to supply and demand conditions. They are intended to eliminate ________________ inflation and the downward rigidity of wages and prices when there is *(unemployment/full employment)* .

12.87

Whether any such actions are taken to deal with the unemployment-inflation trade-off, it is clear that monetary and fiscal policy *(can/cannot)* be used to control aggregate demand and thereby help avoid or eliminate unemployment or demand-pull inflation. But as long as a trade-off exists, monetary and fiscal policy *(can/cannot)* be expected to eliminate completely both unemployment and inflation.

12.88

In the past few years, the dilemma facing policy makers has become more dramatic. The rate of inflation has been much higher than was the case for previous periods with comparable unemployment rates. Some economists believe that this change was the result of a change in expectations. Others think it was due to structural changes in the economy that increased excess demand in some sectors with rising prices in those sectors and increased excess supply in other sectors without offsetting falling prices in those sectors. Whether it is one or both of these factors cannot yet be determined for certain, but it seems evident that the curve shown in Figure 12.3 has shifted to the *(right/left)*
Hopefully, the shift is a temporary one.

REVIEW QUESTIONS

12.1

Last year, output per worker in the carpet industry was 3 percent higher than the year before. The union, through collective bargaining, was able to obtain a 3 percent increase in wages. If nonlabor costs per unit of output remained the same, by how much would it be necessary to raise the price of carpets to keep profit per unit of output from falling?

Answers

86. cost-push · unemployment
87. can · cannot
88. right

a. more than 3 percent
b. 3 percent
c. less than 3 percent, but more than 0 percent
d. 0 percent

Assuming that all last year's higher output of carpets was sold at the previous year's prices, total revenue would have risen by 3 percent, the productivity increase. Thus, all costs, that is, wages, interest and profit, could have risen by 3 percent, and the previous year's relative factor returns would have remained unaltered. Because wages are less than 100 percent of factor returns, and because nonlabor costs per unit of output remained unchanged, the 3 percent gain in productivity made possible a 3 percent gain in wages and a 3 percent increase in profit without a price increase. Using a numerical example could clarify this point and help avoid a common error. The correct response is d.

12.2
If this year the economy is at full employment with a rate of inflation as expected for a fully employed economy and if there are no autonomous changes in aggregate demand, then it is likely that next year there will be:

a. full employment with reasonable price stability, because aggregate demand and consequently GNP will remain unchanged.
b. higher unemployment with less inflation because the usual increase in potential GNP can be expected to remain unchanged.
c. full employment with more inflation because the growth in potential GNP will induce greater consumption and aggregate demand.
d. unemployment with more inflation because the fact that the economy was at full employment this year will result in greater demands for wage increases.

If there are no autonomous increases in aggregate demand, actual GNP can be expected to remain unchanged. Potential GNP can be expected, as usual, to increase from this year to the next as a result of this year's investment in new capital goods and this year's growth in the labor force. Consequently, a gap between actual and potential GNP can be expected to develop. This output gap would mean higher unemployment, which in turn, because of the downward slope in the trade-off between unemployment and inflation, would mean less inflation. The correct answer is b.

12.3
Which of the following will be true when inflation occurs, even though the economy is below full employment?

1. Aggregate demand exceeds potential GNP.
2. Increases in wages or other income payments exceed factor productivity increases.
3. Monetary and fiscal policy cannot achieve price stability without worsening the unemployment problem.
   a. 1 and 2 only
   b. 1 and 3 only
   c. 2 and 3 only
   d. 1, 2, and 3

When the economy is below full employment, aggregate demand is below potential GNP by definition. Therefore, statement 1 cannot be true. Inflation occurs because of rising unit costs when the economy is below full unemployment. It must be true that the price of some factor of production must be rising faster than the productivity of that factor. And, if monetary and fiscal policy were used to reduce aggregate demand in an attempt to fight inflation, the result would have to be a widening gap between actual and potential GNP and a worsening of the unemployment problem. The correct response is c.

12.4

In response to expansionary monetary and fiscal policy, national income has risen to an all-time high, unemployment has fallen to its lowest level in three years, and the rate of inflation, though somewhat higher than in recent years, is only slightly above the historical average. A leading economist has proposed that for the coming year the government reduce income taxes or increase its spending. What can be inferred about the economist's policy objectives?

a. He seeks lower unemployment even at the expense of a higher rate of inflation.
b. He seeks a lower inflation rate even at the expense of higher unemployment.
c. He seeks lower unemployment and lower interest rates.
d. He seeks higher unemployment and higher interest rates.

As aggregate demand has expanded relative to aggregate supply, the difference between actual and potential output has diminished—we know this because the level of unemployment has fallen. If aggregate demand were increased at a faster rate, the unemployment rate would become even lower. It is expected, however, that the rate of inflation, which has risen somewhat as unemployment has fallen, would increase even more at still lower unemployment levels. The economist obviously feels that the marginal benefit from the lower unemployment exceeds the marginal cost of higher inflation. The correct response is a.